LANGUAGE ARTS

WILLIAM & MARY

THE CENTER FOR GIFTED EDUCATION

Guide to Teaching a Language Arts Curriculum for High-Ability Learners

Second Edition

Setting the Standards for Over Twenty Years

A Curriculum for All Seasons!

Kendall Hunt
publishing company

Cover background image photo courtesy of The College of William & Mary.
Cover images left to right: © JupiterImages Corporation, © Shutterstock, Inc.,
© Shutterstock, Inc., © Shutterstock, Inc.

Kendall Hunt publishing company

www.kendallhunt.com
Send all inquiries to:
4050 Westmark Drive
Dubuque, IA 52004-1840
1-800-542-6657

Center for Gifted Education
College of William & Mary
PO Box 8795
Williamsburg, VA 23187-8795
757-221-2362
www.cfge.wm.edu

Funded by the Jacob K. Javits Program, United States Department of Education, under a subcontract from the Washington-Saratoga-Warren-Hamilton-Essex BOCES, Saratoga Springs, New York.

ISBN 978-0-7575-6483-3

Printed in the United States of America

Contents

SECTION 6

Frequently Asked Questions About the William & Mary Language Arts Curriculum

SECTION 7

Language Arts Resources for Teachers

Acknowledgments

Center for Gifted Education Staff

Second Edition

Dr. Joyce VanTassel-Baska, *Executive Director and Guide Author*
Dr. Kimberley Chandler, *Curriculum Director*
Meredith Roberson, *Graduate Assistant*
Kimberley Thoresen, *Graduate Assistant*

First Edition

Dr. Joyce VanTassel-Baska, *Project Director*
Dana T. Johnson, *Project Manager*
Linda Neal Boyce, *Project Consultant*
Dr. Catherine A. Little, *Project Consultant*

Introduction to the William & Mary Center for Gifted Education Units

SECTION 1

Utilization of Unit Materials

What Is the William & Mary Center for Gifted Education Language Arts Curriculum?

The William & Mary language arts curriculum is an integrated program of study that emphasizes all four strands of language arts instruction: literature, writing, oral communication, and language study. Moreover, because the program is designed for high-ability learners, there is a strong emphasis on higher level thinking and concept development within the language arts curriculum and across other disciplines. The program may be implemented as a core language arts experience and supplemented as necessary with other materials. The units cover a range of grade levels, encompassing elementary through high school. Each unit represents a semester of work.

How Do the Units Relate to Curriculum Reform?

The William & Mary units were developed using appropriate curriculum dimensions for high-ability students but also using design features of curriculum reform. Specifically, the units employ the following emphases:

- *Meaning-based:* emphasizing depth over breadth, concepts over facts, and grounded in real world issues and problems that today's students care about or need to understand.
- *Higher order thinking:* treating thinking skills as integral to all content areas and providing students with opportunities to demonstrate their understanding of them through strategies such as concept webbing, persuasive writing, and conducting research.
- *Intra- and interdisciplinary connections:* using overarching concepts, issues, and themes as the organizers for making connections between areas of study.
- *Metacognition:* reflecting on one's own learning processes and consciously planning, monitoring, and assessing learning for efficient and effective use of time and resources.
- *Habits of mind:* cultivating modes of thinking that resemble those of professionals in various fields with respect to skills, predispositions, and attitudes.
- *Active learning and problem solving:* putting students in charge of their own learning—finding out what they know, what they don't know, and what they need to know.
- *Concept-based:* organizing activities around a broad, interdisciplinary concept that promotes deep thinking and substantive connections within and across disciplines.
- *Multiculturalism and globalism:* recognizing that other countries and cultures have made significant contributions to the progress of humankind in many areas. Moreover, curriculum should reflect in an equitable way the contributions of minority groups comprising America today through activities, strategies, and materials.

- *Technology-relevant:* using various new technologies as tools for the learning process, from doing library research via the Internet, to composing using a word processor, to communicating with students across the world by e-mail.
- *Learner outcomes of significance:* setting expectations for learning segments at targeted grade levels that reflect the priorities of the new curriculum for being broad-based, conceptual, and relevant to real-world application.
- *Authentic assessment:* tapping into what students know as a result of meaningful instruction, using approaches such as portfolios and performance-based activities.

How Do the Units Relate to Literacy Research?

Current national standards call for student mastery of general as well as specific academic concepts and skills (National Research Council, 1996) based on a sound foundation of functional literacy (National Institute of Child Health and Human Development [NICHHD], 2000). Moreover, recent reports on authentic education stress the need for students to engage in higher order thinking, critical analysis, substantive course work, and depth, synthesis, and integration of learning within environments that provide social and emotional support for achievement (Newman, Bryk, & Nagaoka, 2001). As such, the current educational literature describes a need for structured and consecutively tiered or laddered levels of academic attainment, rising from basic literacy rungs to advanced higher level rungs.

In a review of 16 reciprocal teaching studies, Rosenshine and Meister (1994) found that careful scaffolding of instruction was central to enhancing literacy, and that even a single strategic approach (e.g., having students ask questions about text) was sufficient to improve reading comprehension. The role of strategic instruction is critically important, especially at the middle school level (Schorzman & Cheek, 2004), for all ability groups (Applebee, Langer, Nystrand, & Gamoran, 2003), as well as for students with learning disabilities (Gersten, Fuchs, Williams, & Baker, 2001). Also, the use of instructional routines has been found useful for learning disabled students (Deshler et al., 2001). Other researchers found that open discussion among peers was an essential strategy for improving literacy (Applebee et al., 2003; Alvermann et al., 1996). In several studies, scaffolded instruction and peer interaction combined resulted in greater gains in reading comprehension than either approach alone (Hamel & Smith, 1998; Langer, 2001).

Augmentation of reading comprehension strategies with writing instruction is yet another approach that has improved reading comprehension significantly (Langer, 1999). In a study investigating the efficacy of writing instruction, Applebee and Langer (2006) found that 67% of eighth-grade students are expected to write an hour or less a week, thus raising the question of insufficient writing time as a factor in literacy underdevelopment.

Instructional scaffolding that embeds strategic instruction in text reading, as described above, has been shown to enhance reading comprehension (Fielding & Pearson, 1994; Villaume & Brabham, 2002). Moreover, teachers who emphasize higher order thinking among their students thoughtfully employ reflective questioning strategies and provide tasks that promote greater reading growth (Knapp et al., 1995; Taylor, Pearson, Peterson, & Rodriguez, 2003).

Although there has been a relatively strong instructional emphasis on phonemic awareness, phonics, and the alphabetic principles (Chall, 2000; Snow, Burns, &

Griffin, 1998), considerably less attention has been given to reading comprehension (Boulineau, Fore, Hagan-Burke, & Burke, 2004; Gersten et al., 2001), and still less attention has been paid to critical thinking among at-risk learners (Tindal & Nolet, 1995). Yet as the student population becomes more diverse in schools and as our concept of literacy broadens (Phelps, 2005), it is essential that educators differentiate instruction effectively to better address learner needs (VanTassel-Baska, 2003).

How Does the William & Mary Curriculum Apply the General Literacy Research?

The William & Mary Language Arts Units build on this foundation of research in general education in several ways:

1. The units all employ instructional scaffolds in the form of graphic organizers to help students grapple with textual meaning and organize their thinking before speaking or writing.
2. The units focus on moving students through reading comprehension to higher level thinking through the use of questions and activities that encourage making meaning in a collaborative and open classroom context.
3. The units provide multicultural materials for reading such that all students experience the richness and complexity of works by our best authors, representing African American, Hispanic American, and Asian American cultures. Works by diverse authors cut across genres in the units to include poetry, short stories, essays, and novels.
4. The units integrate reading and writing activities in a seamless way that allows students to explore text in greater depth to enhance comprehension and to practice various writing models, including persuasive and narrative.

How Do the Units Relate to General Program Approaches in Teaching Reading and Language Arts?

Four instructional programs have principles that fit well with the William & Mary units. These four approaches are highlighted in this section: the Four-Blocks® literacy model, balanced literacy, and silent sustained reading (SSR). The Accelerated Reader™ program is also discussed, relative to it use with gifted students.

The Four-Blocks® Literacy Model

A general approach to teaching language arts may be seen in the Four-Blocks® literacy model, used as a framework for language arts instruction in many schools.

Guided Reading

The first block of the Four-Blocks® literacy model is guided reading. Guided reading focuses on teaching students the skills and strategies they need to comprehend text. In the William & Mary units, this is accomplished through the use of guided questions and the Literature Web Model. Both are provided to develop students' use of skills and strategies needed to comprehend the various texts. Although the Literature Web is completed individually, it is through the discussion of the text and the Literature Web that students gain a better understanding of the text. Questions asked in the William & Mary units are developed for use in small groups or whole class groups.

The William & Mary language arts units may also be adapted for use in literature circles. Literature circles promote discussion and sharing of ideas in small, flexible groups. These groups form based on the students' choices of novels and disband after the novels are finished. Literature circle groups seek to increase student comprehension of a book through thoughtful discussion.

The texts used in William & Mary units may easily be used in this format.

Groups for literature circles can be formed in a variety of ways. Groups can be formed to read self-selected novels outside of class in conjunction with the unit, or they can be formed to discuss the novels read by all students in the class. Groups should be formed to facilitate a collection of diverse opinions and experiences in order to promote genuine conversation (Daniels, 2002).

Self-Selected Texts

The self-selected text component of the Four-Blocks® literacy model encourages students to choose their own reading material, which helps students develop a sense of enjoyment that comes from reading. In the William & Mary units, students can select reading material from a list or collection of materials for either a research project or reading to be completed at home. In some units, students select a specific reading in a particular genre, such as autobiographies of writers.

All the literature in the unit is selected based on specific criteria to ensure that reading materials are advanced. Literature selection is based on the criteria suggested by Baskin and Harris (1980) and multicultural literature is selected based on criteria suggested by Miller-Lachmann (1992).

Writing

The writing component of the Four-Blocks® literacy model engages students in mini-lessons and a writer's workshop process. Writer's workshop consists of five steps: prewriting, drafting, revising, editing, and publishing. Similarly, the William & Mary units use the Writing Process Model to improve student writing of key pieces. During the revision process, the student, peers, and the teacher provide input for the work. The student's work is peer- and self-assessed throughout the process. In all of the William & Mary units, there is a strong emphasis on persuasive writing. Students are given a preassessment, which can help teachers determine what skills or processes need to be reviewed or retaught to students. The postassessment for persuasive writing allows students and teachers to see growth in the persuasive writing elements of data, claim, and warrant.

Working with Words

The working with words component of the Four-Blocks® literacy model focuses on teaching and improving students' word attack skills. These are the skills students need to decode new words, recognize patterns in spelling, and learn high-frequency words. The William & Mary units address these skills by having students use a Vocabulary Web to build their vocabulary. Students not only find a word's definition but also synonyms, antonyms, and etymological information. This allows students to make connections with this new word to their existing vocabulary, and also provides students with a way to decode meanings of more complex words. By studying the etymological information of new words, students will be able to apply those stems or root words to new vocabulary, thus allowing them to decode the meanings of longer and more complex words. Students will also begin to see the relationships and patterns among words that were previously overlooked.

Word walls and studies of word families are tools that, when used in conjunction with the Vocabulary Web, can strengthen students' vocabulary and word attack skills (Brabham & Villaume, 2001). The purpose of the word wall is for students to gain mastery of new words or concepts. In order for word walls to be effective, teachers must also encourage students to use these new words or concepts in their daily language. Study of word families can also effectively strengthen students' vocabulary and word attack skills.

Balanced Literacy

A balanced literacy approach implies that students are exposed to the full array of effective strategies that readers and writers use. All William & Mary curriculum units incorporate the use of multiple teaching/learning models. These models are explicitly taught to students and then used with a variety of literature pieces. Each one is modeled by the teacher and as the unit progresses, students move from being provided with high levels of teacher support to independence. This method aligns with the gradual release of responsibility model by Pearson and Gallagher (1983), where learners go from having a strategic activity modeled, to shared and guided activities, and finally to independent applications of a new skill or process (Mahurt, Metcalfe, & Gwyther, 2007, p. 3).

The Literature Web, Vocabulary Web, Taba's Model of Concept Development, Paul's Elements of Reasoning Model, the Hamburger Model, the Dagwood Model, and Research Model are incorporated in all of the William & Mary language arts units.

The Literature Web is comprised of five components: key words, feelings, images and symbols, structure, and ideas. Students are encouraged to discuss these five components, and also to relate their personal responses to elements in the literature. The Literature Web can be used as a discussion tool as well.

The Vocabulary Web is designed to encourage students to explore words in greater depth in order to develop stronger vocabularies. Students study the meaning of the word as well as synonyms, antonyms, and the etymological information. This allows students to make connections to prior vocabulary words and also allows them to develop their knowledge of stem or root words.

Taba's Model of Concept Development is used to teach students the overarching concept in each unit. Students list examples and nonexamples, categorize examples, and then create generalizations relating to the concept. Students are then asked throughout the unit to apply these generalizations to various types of literature, writing, and their own lives.

Paul's Reasoning Model is used to develop students' critical thinking skills. The Reasoning Model consists of eight elements: issue, purpose, point of view, evidence, concepts, assumptions, inferences, and implications. Students use the Elements of Reasoning to develop and evaluate arguments on various issues. This is usually used in conjunction with persuasive writing in the William & Mary units.

The Hamburger and Dagwood Models are persuasive writing models. The Hamburger Model is used for experienced writers; a primary adaptation of this model has also been created for beginning writers. The Dagwood Model is used for advanced writers. The models guide students in creating either a paragraph or essay. Students start by stating their point of view followed by providing three reasons and a conclusion. The Hamburger Model requires students to elaborate on their three reasons, while the Dagwood Model also requires students to present opposing points of view and provide support from literature for their perspectives.

The Research Model guides students through the research process. The elements of this model are based on the Elements of Reasoning. The eight components of the Research Model are as follows: identifying the issue or problem, identifying points of views or arguments through information sources, forming questions, gathering evidence, manipulating and transforming data, drawing conclusions and making inferences, determining implications and consequences, and communicating findings.

In balanced literacy instruction, there are core components employed that can be applied through the William & Mary units.

- **Opportunities for student modeling and sharing of standard-setting, proficient reading and writing work**
  Throughout the William & Mary units, students are exposed to other students' work through assessment of writing. During the writing process, students edit as well as assess other students' writing. Students also assess each others' persuasive speeches during the unit. Every unit also contains a research project that students present at the end of the unit. Through structured discussions and Literature Webs, students are exposed to multiple interpretations and responses to different literature.

- **Reading to students (aloud), together with students (shared and guided), and by students (independently), using quality pieces of fiction and nonfiction text**
  The William & Mary language arts units focus on independent reading of quality pieces of fiction. Each piece of literature is reviewed and selected on the basis of criteria suggested by Baskin and Harris (1980). Multicultural literature is also incorporated and selected based on criteria suggested by Miller-Lachmann (1992). Although reading aloud to students is not a component of the language arts units, teachers have the option of using this strategy with students.

- **Oral language development and listening experiences**
  Presentations of research, persuasive writing, and other student-generated work are used in the William & Mary language arts units to develop students' oral language and listening skills. Students listen to classmates' work not only for exposure to proficient writing but also for the purpose of evaluation. Students also assess persuasive speeches during the unit, which helps to strengthen listening skills.

- **Word study instruction and practice to build students' vocabulary, word recognition, spelling, and fluency skills through a developmental process**
  The Vocabulary Web is used as the main component of word study in the William & Mary units. Units from Grades 4 to 9 also incorporate a grammar study section. The focus of the word study in the units is on creating a deeper understanding of interesting and complex words through the use of the Vocabulary Web. Grammar components emphasize the development of understanding form, function, and the selective combination of words to create meaning.

- **Independent reading and writing to build fluency and provide for creativity and choice**
  There are many opportunities for independent reading in the William & Mary units. Most of the reading is done independently both outside and in class. During the unit, students read at least one novel at home in addition to other in-class books and readings. Students also have journals they complete on their novels outside of class. This not only provides students practice responding to literature but also allows for student choice in writing. Students are required to write a response after a certain number of pages; the guidelines for their responses are flexible.

- **Expository and narrative reading and writing experiences threaded throughout all the content areas**
  The writing experiences in the William & Mary units focus on persuasive writing, although extensions are provided that allow for other types of writing opportunities.

- **Multiple opportunities for engagement, inquiry, and expression through various reading and writing groupings, formats, resources, and projects**
  Throughout the William & Mary language arts units, students are engaged with various types of reading and writing opportunities. These units can also be incorporated in various classroom grouping settings. Comments relating to implementation for various grouping models are included later in this section of the guide.

- **Multiple and varied student assessments to drive instruction**
  Multiple assessments are incorporated into each unit. Students are given a pre- and

postassessment as well as multiple self-, peer, and teacher evaluations throughout the unit. There are also opportunities for informal assessment such as student response journals, student writing portfolios, and student–teacher conferences.

Response to Intervention

The emphasis in recent years on Response to Intervention (RTI) approaches, initiated by special educators to afford more appropriate approaches being used with these learners in literacy classrooms, dovetails well with the basic rationale of the William & Mary units; this rationale acknowledges the need for individualizing and differentiating curriculum and instruction based on the level of the learner. A major emphasis in the RTI model is on diagnosing the level of reading and providing appropriate materials and instruction to promote advancement in the learning process. The pretesting model of the William & Mary units effectively applies this principle and also offers the instructional scaffolding to assist in the process. While RTI is seen as an effective tool for finding students who are not achieving, it works equally well to discern students who are achieving at an above-grade level rate. The differentiation processes are the same; it is the outcomes that vary.

The main features of RTI are (Fuchs & Fuchs, 2007; Mellard & Johnson, 2008):

1. High-quality instruction
2. Research-based instruction
3. Classroom performance via curriculum-based assessments
4. Universal screening for problems in achievement and behavior
5. Continuous progress monitoring
6. Research-based interventions
7. Progress monitoring during interventions
8. Teacher fidelity of implementation assessments

Employment of each of these processes is also critical to ensure that high-ability learners are making adequate progress in their work, showing at least a year's growth for a year spent in school, receiving a differentiated research-based intervention appropriate for their needs, and being tracked for success, and that teachers are faithfully implementing the differentiated plan. The William & Mary units provide a suitable way to employ RTI with the gifted learner.

Sustained Silent Reading

The sustained silent reading approach has been systematically employed in language arts classrooms to provide in-class reading time for students. Fostered by the need to provide more reading time in the curriculum, coupled with research that suggests the process facilitates enhanced reading comprehension, schools have often mandated time in the curriculum for this approach (Gardiner, 2001). Specifically, research suggests that both reading comprehension and vocabulary growth occur for students who read more (Wiesendose & Baker, 1989). The effects are also stronger for students who are allowed to select their own texts and when the program is used for at least six months (Yoon, 2002). Positive attitudes toward reading also appear to develop as a result of the program (Chow & Chou, 2000).

Unfortunately, it is not as effective a process for the gifted reader for the most part, as this student could benefit more from increased time for reading discussion and time to answer a writing prompt. Using silent reading time in a differentiated way for the gifted student greatly enhances the time as a period of learning. Many of the extension activities in the William & Mary units can be used to enhance the learning of the gifted reader.

Accelerated Reader

Accelerated Reader™ (AR) is a computer-based, reading management and motivational system designed to complement existing classroom literacy programs for Grades K–12. AR's goal is to motivate students to read using a grade equivalent (GE) score from a standardized test, such as STAR Reading, coupled with the amount of time the student is able to devote to reading. AR translates GE scores into a zone of proximal development (ZPD) range that is used to determine the level of books from which the student can select.

Students choose books or short stories to read from the school's selected collection of books for which they have AR tests. AR provides extensive lists with thousands of book titles and their corresponding grade levels and point values.

AR software provides comprehension tests featuring 5 to 20 multiple-choice questions. The technology presents test scores and points earned, and keeps records in order to help teachers and parents manage and track a student's attempt to reach his or her goal. The test gives immediate feedback about the number of points earned based on the point value assigned to the book and the number of correct answers on the test.

The AR program is not appropriate for use with gifted learners. Its goal is to interest students in reading more books and answering factual questions about them to verify their having read the selection. The choice of literature is based on grade level expectations and the questions are too perfunctory to benefit these highly able learners. The computer-based program is best employed with reluctant readers who need stimulating books to keep them motivated at a self-pace that they can manage effectively (Peak & Dewalt, 1994; Samuels & Wu, 2004; Vollands, Topping, & Evans, 1999).

What Are the Goals of the William & Mary Curriculum?

The goals for the majority of the language arts curriculum units are as follows:

- To develop analytical and interpretive skills in literature.
- To develop persuasive writing skills.
- To develop linguistic competency.
- To develop listening/oral communication skills.
- To develop reasoning skills in the language arts.
- To understand the concept of change.

Additional focuses included in some of the units are analogical reasoning skills, the analysis of figurative language, the concept of utopia, and the concept of cyclical change.

The Integrated Curriculum Model

The Integrated Curriculum Model (ICM), a theoretical model of curriculum design for gifted learners (see Figure 1-1), emphasizes the integration of advanced content, higher order thinking processes, and connections to overarching themes and issues as the foundation for curriculum development. The greatest student learning occurs when emphasis is given to each of these dimensions within a given curriculum unit (VanTassel-Baska, 1986). The ICM was derived from the key characteristics of gifted students and how curriculum may be designed to best match those characteristics. For example, because gifted students are precocious learners, advanced content within a given subject area provides opportunities for new learning. Because gifted learners have complex thinking capacities, the provision of a curriculum that helps gifted students reason through situations and think critically about subject matter enhances engagement and creative production. Moreover, because many gifted students thrive on making connections, the focus on overarching issues, themes, and concepts elevates their

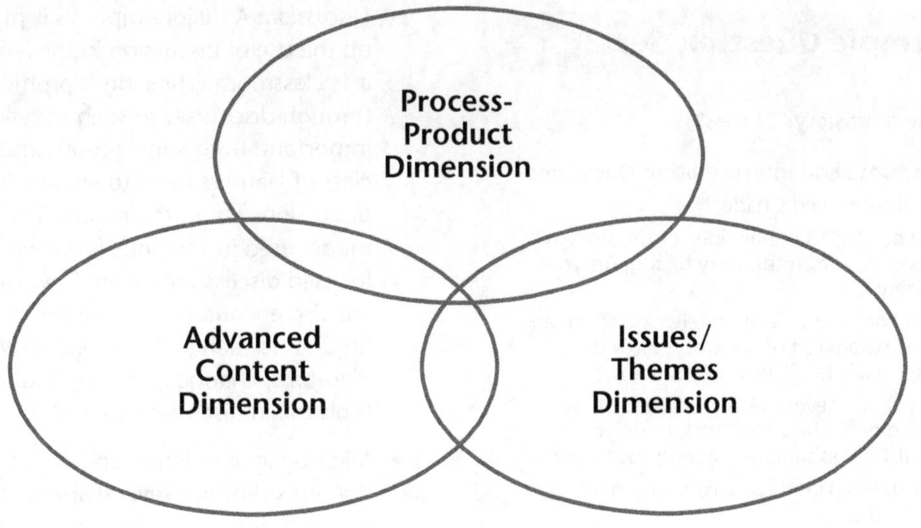

Figure 1-1: Integrated Curriculum Model

VanTassel-Baska, 1986

understanding of the real world and how it works. These three components of the ICM (advanced content, processes/products, and overarching issues, themes, and concepts) have comprised the framework for curriculum design and differentiation (VanTassel-Baska, 1995) in all of the William & Mary units of study. Each William & Mary unit is organized around the Integrated Curriculum Model (ICM) that is carefully mapped on specific lessons. To honor this integrated approach, teachers need to be flexible in the actual number of sessions that students may need in order to work through the unit. It is important that all lessons are taught in some depth to ensure that the major goals and unit outcomes are sufficiently addressed.

Anatomy of a Language Arts Unit

EACH UNIT CONTAINS the following components:

- *Curriculum framework:* The set of unit goals and outcomes is stated for easy reference.
- *Implementation guide:* Comprehensive support for administering the units in various classroom settings as well as effectively implementing the various teaching models and assessment tools is provided in a special section.
- *Lesson plans:* A set of lesson plans is presented, each with information about instructional purpose, materials needed, activities, questions, and assessment ideas.
- *Assessment:* Assessment approaches in the unit include pre–post reading and writing performance tasks, pre–post grammar tests, writing assessments, research presentation assessments, portfolio work to be collected and assessed in each lesson, and a final assessment that measures major unit objectives.
- *References:* The set of specific references that may be useful for implementing the unit may be found at the end of each unit.

Language Arts Teaching Strategies

All of the units emphasize the following strategies:

- *Questions:* Questions are organized to address important aspects of unit learning. They focus on understanding change, on the Elements of Reasoning, and on literary response and interpretation. Thus, typically, questions are grouped within lessons according to those designations as in the example on the next page.

Sample Question Set

(Based on the short story "Charles")

Literary Response and Interpretation Questions

- Why does Laurie need Charles?
- What do you think the main idea of the story is? Provide evidence from the story to support your point of view.
- What does the phrase "elaborately casual" mean in the third paragraph of the story? How does the mother really feel? How do you know?
- Why does Laurie never talk about what he himself did at school? What clues do you have about Charles's identity during the story?
- Why are Laurie's parents so anxious to meet Charles's mother?
- What does Laurie's father mean when he says, "I don't see how they could hold a PTA meeting without Charles's mother"?
- How effective was the ending of the story? Explain your response.
- The story reports what happened each day at Laurie's house as he described Charles's behavior. What do you think conversations were like at the other kindergartners' houses? Laurie's mother went to the meeting anxious to meet Charles's mother. What might the other mothers have been thinking? How do you think Laurie's mother's perceptions of the other mothers changed after she spoke to the teacher?
- What might be another title for this story? Give several reasons for your response.

Reasoning Questions

- Who is Charles? Give **evidence** from the story to support your opinion.
- What **point of view** do Laurie's parents have about Charles?
- What can you **infer** about Laurie's feelings about his experiences, based on events in the story? Give **evidence** from the story for your ideas.
- What can you **infer** about Laurie's adjustment to kindergarten from his teacher's comment, "We had a little trouble adjusting, the first week or so, but now he's a fine little helper. With occasional lapses, of course."

Change Questions

- How does Charles's behavior **change** in the story? Why does it change?
- How do the generalizations about **change** relate to this story?

- *Discussion:* A major emphasis is placed on the use of discussion in the language arts classroom. Thinking is promoted best through discourse, so such conversation is important. Both small groups and the whole class of learners need to engage in frequent discussions about their work. The questioning model used in the units is one way to ensure a focused discussion lesson. However, teachers are also encouraged to use the graphic organizers such as the Literature Web, Venn diagrams, change matrices, and other such tools to aid discussion as well.
- *Metacognition:* Metacognition is treated in the units through several approaches. The research project provides an opportunity for students to plan, monitor, and assess their progress on a given issue. Moreover, response journals allow students to reflect on their learning experiences after selected lessons.
- *Concept teaching:* Teaching the concept of change is systematically encouraged in the unit through specific lessons. In addition, teachers are encouraged to post the generalizations about change in the classroom and to have students extemporaneously comment on how change is relevant as they progress through the unit.
- *Higher level thinking:* The deliberate use of the Paul Reasoning Model provides a way for the units to focus on higher level thinking. Teachers may use the model in all aspects of unit implementation.
- *Communication skills:* The program stresses the equal importance of written and oral communication skills. Activities that promote the use of these skills are embedded throughout the units of study.

How May the Units Be Used with Various Grouping Models?

The units have been implemented in a variety of grouping settings, including heterogeneous classrooms, pull-out programs, and self-contained gifted classes. Based on feedback from national pilots, we suggest that school districts employ their existing grouping approach to teach the unit the first time. Based on individual district results from the first year of implementation, decisions about modifying grouping procedures may be explored.

A number of different grouping models may be utilized to teach the William & Mary language arts units of study. We recommend the use of flexible grouping as the best approach that allows students to move in and out of groups based on need and their readiness to be involved in various aspects of the unit in the regular classroom. As we know from research, however, more sustained grouping of the gifted and high-ability learners together is likely to enhance the impact of the comprehensive integrated benefits of the units.

Heterogeneous Classrooms

The units may be taught in a heterogeneous setting as long as flexible grouping is employed. At a minimum, students should be grouped by reading levels so that the William & Mary advanced reading selections may be employed with the top reading group. The district reading selections may be used with on-level readers. Special education teachers may wish to make reading assignments for learning disabled and other students identified for special education services. All groups will benefit from the teaching and learning models in the curriculum; they should be used regardless of the reading selections chosen.

Cluster Grouping

A cluster grouping model should be workable with the units if strong readers are clustered regularly for instruction in the unit. Daily work in reading clusters is advisable for at least an hour to sustain the various elements involved in delivering a unit of study. Cluster groups should have no more than four to five students to maximize the opportunity for discussion. If more students qualify for the cluster, then two groups could be formed to keep group size smaller.

Pull-Out Grouping

Use of the units in pull-out grouping programs is highly effective as long as the time spent in the pull-out setting can accommodate the parameters of the unit. A minimum recommended two hours per week as the timeframe for unit implementation is warranted, whether on one day or across multiple days a week. The entire unit of study would take at least a semester to implement on this model.

Special Classes (Honors) in Language Arts

At the middle school level and even earlier, the use of the units in a daily honors language arts program is an ideal setting for implementation. It allows for the comprehensiveness and integrated quality of the units to be appreciated and understood. Used on a daily basis, one unit could be used for about nine weeks, using appropriate supplements to the core curriculum. Subgrouping of students within the class for discussions and projects should be done routinely to accommodate different reading levels, rates, and interests.

Full-Time Classes for the Gifted at Elementary Level/Special Schools for the Gifted

This grouping model allows for the fullest implementation of the units in an interdisciplinary setting where extension projects might easily be implemented and connections to other subjects made more easily. Unit connections to social studies, math, science, and the arts can be explored more thoroughly, using the concept of change and the Reasoning Model as the threads that connect the subject areas together. Application of the other models may also be relevant to enhance a broader application of the entire set of learning tools.

What Is the Scope and Sequence for These Language Arts Units?

The definitional structure of scope and sequence may be found in the curriculum work of VanTassel-Baska (1992). Scope refers to the extensiveness of the curriculum experiences across a predetermined period of time. The determination of scope hinges on the value attached to what is being taught. For purposes of the William and Mary Center for Gifted Education curriculum, the scope of the curriculum is limited to core concepts and units of study usable for 9 to 18 weeks of full-time instruction. Sequence refers to the order in which the desired curriculum experiences will be taught and learned. For purposes of this curriculum, the order was established around student progression of knowledge, skills, and concepts from Grades 1 through 12. Individual units have been targeted for use at specific grade level clusters over the span of years.

The following list illustrates how the units allow students to progress over the years the units are used:

1. Concept learning becomes more advanced as new and more complex applications are made in each succeeding unit.
2. Reasoning becomes more complex as students apply more aspects of the Paul Reasoning Model in their work.
3. The choice of literature becomes more advanced in each unit.
4. Applications in all the language arts areas become more in-depth, complex, and rigorous.

Many school districts choose to use a series of the language arts units across elementary, middle, and high school years. Use of different units across grade levels is encouraged to provide multiple applications of the concept of change, the use of the reasoning process, and the enhancement of language arts skills.

The William & Mary curriculum units are all organized around a common framework that has the same set of goals and outcomes at each level. The level of difficulty and complexity of the texts read are the elements that differ in each unit. The same teaching and learning models are used throughout the units to enhance deeper understanding of text and to provide easy transference for the learner. The models are meant to become automatic for learners over time. Given the level of thought required to apply them, even gifted learners would require multiple years to reach a comfortable degree of automaticity. Thus the repetition proves to be useful in enhancing long-term learning of higher level material.

Sequencing issues in the units do occur in certain aspects of implementation. The literature is calibrated to become more advanced and complex as students progress to higher grade levels. Moving from complex picture books to chapter books to novels is a natural progression in form that is employed. Short stories and poetry with increasing complexity in the selections chosen are used throughout the units. As students mature, the research projects become more elaborate, real world, and issue-based. Students also have more choices to make in the projects as they progress through the grade levels. The teaching of grammar in a formal way does not begin until Grade 4. From that time, through Grade 9, a self-study packet is used to guide readers independently through a set of exercises that are sequenced for form, function, and selective combination of words. A pre- and postassessment allow students and teachers to judge what material needs to be retaught each year.

The following example provides one illustration of sequencing the units for use with gifted learners over time in multiple grade levels.

Grade Level	Unit Title
1-2	*Beyond Words*
2-3	*Journeys and Destinations*
4-5	*Literary Reflections*
4-6	*Patterns of Change*
5-6	*Autobiographies and Memoirs*
6-7	*Persuasion*
7-9	*Utopia*
7-9	*The 1940s: A Decade of Change*
8-10	*Threads of Change in 19th Century American Literature*
10-12	*Change Through Choices*

How Should the William & Mary Units Be Used in Gifted Programs?

The role of the William & Mary units in a program for high-ability learners is foundational for language arts instruction. They represent the core program around which supplementary materials may be added. Specifically, the material may be supplemented with writing, spelling, and additional reading selections. The teaching and learning models that form the basis for the professional development program should be employed throughout each year of language arts instruction.

It is probably wise to teach only one William & Mary unit per year as they are time-consuming to teach and rich in detail and extensions that students may complete. Program supplementary materials like Junior Great Books and Michael Thompson's vocabulary and grammar work are excellent for extending key unit goals in reading, writing, speaking, and mastering new vocabulary and grammatical principles.

When adopting the units as core curriculum, districts are advised to gain the approval of texts through the standard approach used in the district as several texts are deliberately chosen for their intellectual content, advanced level, and multicultural representation. Alignment charts should be consulted to show the relationship of the William & Mary curriculum to language arts standards in the district and state. The units were originally aligned to the National Language Arts Standards project and later aligned in numerous states in a deliberate way. A strong program for the gifted learner should always include:

- **Differentiated curriculum based on research-based materials**
  We no longer need to depend on every teacher writing curriculum for gifted students. Rather, over the past decade, we have seen new curricula that are research-based be made available through the federal Javits program. This material, coupled with older materials that have been successfully used with gifted learners, should comprise the curriculum used with gifted learners in language arts.
- **Strategies that are high powered**
  Given our new research on cognitive learning strategies, we now know that teachers can access more approaches to teaching that elevate instruction to higher levels of thought. Graphic organizers, well-conceptualized and implemented, can make a big difference in raising learning to new heights not just for the gifted student, but for all students.
- **Assessment that is differentiated**
  Assessments for gifted learners have to show value-added learning that extend beyond the annual state testing program and assess authentic learning in a subject area that is truly advanced. The curriculum-based assessments in the William & Mary units do just that. By using a pre–post format, students demonstrate their critical thinking ability applied to text comprehension, writing, presentation, and research venues.

On the following page is an example of how a language arts program may be designed at the fourth-grade level, incorporating a William & Mary unit and utilizing other resources:

Language Arts Program for Gifted Students

Core	Supplementary Materials
Literary Reflections (18-week duration)	*Junior Great Books* Touchstones (reading and discussions) Johns Hopkins Writing Workshop Model
Writing	*Writing Source 2000* (English) *Caesar's English* (vocabulary and Latin) *Words Their Way* (spelling) *Magic Lens* (grammar)
Core novels and short story selections from the basal reader	
Core novels, based on district's reading lists Use of Navigators (see www.cfge.wm.edu) for differentiation (*Sarah Plain & Tall; Tuck Everlasting; Bridge to Terabithia*)	

Summary

Final words to teachers implementing the units:

1. The units have been organized in a highly integrated way. Please try to implement them as fully as possible.
2. Teachers report that the units require "teacher learning" in order to be implemented effectively. Put in the time before beginning to teach the unit so that your students benefit optimally from the unit experience.
3. New teachers report great success in using the lesson plans because they are sufficiently detailed without being scripted. Use the material already prepared for you when possible.
4. Remember that change is challenging ... but also necessary for growth and development. Enjoy the rigor and challenge!

Differentiation for High-Ability Learners

The William & Mary Center for Gifted Education language arts curriculum was developed with a consideration of the characteristics and needs of high-ability learners. The following chart illustrates this relationship:

High-Ability Learner Characteristics	Corresponding Emphases in the Curriculum
Advanced reading ability	Rich, complex literature selected
Advanced vocabulary	Emphasis on vocabulary development through the investigation of etymology, antonyms, synonyms, and related words
Abstract reasoning skills	High-level reasoning in discussion of literature, writing assignments, and oral presentations
Ability to make connections	Thematic organization of curriculum
Power of concentration	Focus on analysis and interpretation of literature Long-term projects and meaningful homework
Concern for moral and ethical issues	Research on issues of significance
Emotional sensitivity	Opportunities for personal response to literature and language
Ability to generate original ideas	Generative project work

The unit contains advanced reading selections and presents challenging activities at increased levels of complexity, all essential curriculum elements for high-ability learners. Specific adaptations made throughout the unit to accommodate these learners include the following:

1. The literature selected for the unit meets the specific criteria for high-ability learners suggested by Baskin and Harris (1980). A detailed description of these criteria follows:
   - The language used in books for the gifted should be rich, varied, precise, complex, and exciting, because language is the instrument for the reception and expression of thought.
   - Books should be chosen with a consideration of their open-endedness, their capacity to inspire contemplative behavior, such as through techniques of judging time sequences, shifting narrators, and unusual speech patterns of characters.
   - Books for the gifted should be complex enough to elicit interpretive and evaluative behaviors from readers.
   - Books for the gifted should help them build problem-solving skills and develop methods of productive thinking.
   - Books should provide characters as role models for emulation.
   - Books should be broad-based in form, from picture books to folktales and myths, to nonfiction, to biography, to poetry, to fiction.
2. The inclusion of high-quality multicultural literature adds another dimension of complexity. Criteria for the selection of this literature, based on Miller-Lachmann (1992), follows:
   - *General accuracy:* Works should adhere to high standards of scholarship and authentic portrayal of thoughts and emotions.

- *Avoidance of stereotypes:* Stereotyping occurs when an author assigns general characteristics to a group rather than exploring its members' diversity and individuality.
- *Language:* Language issues include appropriateness to age group, up-to-date terminology, avoidance of loaded words, and authentic use of dialect.
- *Attention to author's perspective:* Perspective includes the author's mind-set, point of view, experience, and values.
- *Currency of facts and interpretation:* Copyright date alone does not assure recent information.
- *Concept of audience:* Some books appeal to general audiences while others consider issues about heritage and cultural values that have special appeal to members of a specific group. The challenge is for authors to develop the reader's empathy.
- *Integration of cultural information:* Cultural information must be presented in a manner consistent with the flow of the story.
- *Balance and multidimensionality:* Books range from presenting an "objective" perspective, which may contain subtle biases, to those stating a particular viewpoint. Readers should have opportunities to see the multidimensionality of characters and cultures.
- *Illustrations:* Issues that relate to text also apply to illustrations; for instance, illustrations must be accurate and up-to-date and without stereotypes.

3. The inquiry model of discussion moves students from initial reactions to analysis and interpretation of a reading or speech. It invites students to consider multiple perspectives.
4. Vocabulary study in the units extends well beyond definitions. It models the study of challenging words including investigation of etymology, antonyms, synonyms, and related words.
5. Consideration of important issues is treated at several levels of sophistication. Individual points of view are supported and argued through techniques of persuasion. Students are also required to consider and address other points of view.
6. Interdisciplinary connections are made in the units not only by integrating the language arts with the "sister" arts of music and visual arts, but also by addressing changes in social, cultural, economic, and political aspects of various societies.
7. Use of a critical thinking model consistently encourages students to focus on the application of important elements of reasoning in their study of literature.

Research Evidence of Effectiveness of the William & Mary Language Arts Units

The first group of curriculum effectiveness studies of the units employed quasi-experimental conditions with teachers across multiple sites and states who volunteered their classrooms for curricular piloting purposes. This phase used curriculum-based assessment techniques to assess pre–post student learning gains in literary analysis and persuasive writing. Experimental groups were predominantly high-ability learners. Comparison groups were gleaned from the same districts and were selected according to student ability and socioeconomic status (SES) considerations (VanTassel-Baska, Zuo, Avery, & Little, 2002; VanTassel-Baska, Johnson, Hughes, & Boyce, 1996).

Across all units of study, the programmatic goals consistently have included (a) developing student understanding of the concept of change; (b) developing literary analysis and interpretation, persuasive writing skills, and linguistic competency skills; and (c) promoting the reasoning process. Specific learning outcomes have been aligned with the intent of the National Council of Teachers of English and the

International Reading Association standards that advocate for substantive content coverage, high-level thinking, and mastery of meaningful language arts skills. The studies conducted thus far have focused on student application of literary analysis and interpretation, persuasive writing, and linguistic competency (VanTassel-Baska, Johnson, Hughes, & Boyce, 1996; VanTassel-Baska, Zuo, Avery, & Little, 2002).

Using a quasi-experimental design, selected national school districts have implemented one or more of these units. Posttests were administered after approximately 36 hours of instruction, and between-group analyses were conducted using an ANCOVA to covary pretest differences. Elementary and middle school students from a national network of schools participated in the sample, including volunteer schools from seven states. Implementation involved 2,189 students in experimental and comparison classrooms in nine schools. All participating teachers received implementation training for two to five days. Curriculum effectiveness was assessed on two performance-based instruments modeled after existing instrumentation developed by the National Assessment of Educational Progress in Reading (National Assessment Governing Board, 1992).

The first assessment was a performance-based test of literary analysis and interpretation. This evaluation, modeled on the NAEP assessment in reading (National Assessment Governing Board, 1992) addressed four topics: (a) main idea, (b) analysis of a quote, (c) relationship of the concept of change to selection, and (d) creating a title with a rationale to support it. The second assessment was a performance-based persuasive writing assessment that asked students to develop an argument to support or reject a statement. Both assessments were reviewed for content validity by experts in English and gifted education and were given favorable reviews. Inter-rater reliability estimates for scoring each instrument exceeded .90 for each scorer team (VanTassel-Baska, Zuo, Avery, & Little, 2002).

Participating districts were recruited from summer programs and other training institutes between 1996 and 2000. Guidelines for participation included (a) the designation of an on-site coordinator, (b) involvement of at least one experimental and one comparison class, (c) a written description of general district demographics and program descriptors (i.e., grade level, grouping arrangement, and duration of intervention), and (d) permission from an authorized district official. Posttest analyses were conducted using an ANCOVA that covaried pretest between-group differences. Effect sizes were calculated for all analyses involving comparison groups.

The four William & Mary units utilized in the study produced significant pre–post student gains and significant differences between the experimental and comparison groups ($p < .001$); effect sizes were very high for persuasive writing at 2.42, and were high for literary analysis at .70. Repeated exposure to the units produced significant gains as well ($p < .05$). Low SES students showed significant gains in both literary analysis and interpretation and persuasive writing with moderate to high effect sizes ($p < .001$). Gender differences were small. A subsample analysis from one of the school districts that targeted low-socioeconomic learners for intervention found that gains in persuasive writing were greater with this population than for the rest of the sample, suggesting the potential use of the curriculum with students from low-socioeconomic backgrounds. Further analysis of student responses from the field-test sample revealed that more than 50% of the students had room to grow in higher level skill categories, such as elaboration and interpretation, suggesting that the curriculum was sufficiently challenging and offered growth opportunities for high-ability learners.

Teacher Use and Effectiveness in Implementation

Although enhanced student learning is the primary indicator of curriculum effectiveness, teachers' favorable experiences with materials and related instructional strategies are also important. Such experiences support teacher acceptance of the materials, which have contributed to their sustained use over time. Teacher acceptance was evaluated and found to be high in respect to curriculum elements employed, challenge, and reuse (VanTassel-Baska, Johnson, Hughes, & Boyce, 1996).

Data were also collected on changes in teachers' instructional behaviors as a result of both training in, and use of, a differentiated curriculum. Pre–post data using a classroom observation instrument (Classroom Observation Scale-Revised, COS-R, 2005) suggest that experimental teachers showed significant growth patterns in the use of key elements of differentiation (i.e., critical thinking, creative thinking, accommodation to individual differences) across three years of implementation of the William & Mary units of study as compared to comparison teachers not trained in the curriculum (VanTassel-Baska, Feng, et al., 2008).

Longitudinal Findings

A six-year longitudinal study examined the effects of using the William & Mary program in a suburban school district over time and found that gifted student learning in Grades 3 to 5 was enhanced at significant and educationally important levels in critical reading and persuasive writing. Repeated exposure over a two- to three-year period demonstrated increasing achievement patterns, and the majority of stakeholders reported the curriculum to be beneficial and effective (Feng, VanTassel-Baska, Quek, Bai, & O'Neill, 2005). Moreover, a study of selected school districts demonstrated that the curriculum also resulted in positive school change in respect to climate, collegiality, and district policy change (VanTassel-Baska, Avery, Little, & Hughes, 2000).

Based on the growing research evidence on the use of The College of William & Mary's units with gifted learners, the team at William & Mary began a three-year longitudinal study using the curriculum in Title I schools and inclusive classrooms with learners at all levels, including those who were struggling readers (VanTassel-Baska, Bracken, Feng, & Brown, 2006; VanTassel-Baska, Bracken, Feng & Brown, 2009). These studies focused on students in Title I settings using quasi-experimental designs, with random assignment of classrooms to treatment and comparison groups in seven school districts in three states. Most classrooms were inclusive with normal distributions with respect to students' assessed ability. In these studies, special curriculum accommodations were developed to augment the core intervention, including the Jacob's Ladder and Navigator series. Moreover, novel tests were developed during the project to strengthen the assessment of educational outcomes and the generalizability of the findings. These assessments included the Test of Critical Thinking (TCT), used pre–post; the Classroom Observation Scale (COS-R), used to judge and guide fidelity of implementation and differentiation behaviors; and the Student Observation Scale (SOS), used to assess student engagement twice during the implementation period. The curriculum-based assessment was continued in experimental classrooms only (VanTassel-Baska, Bracken, Feng, & Brown, 2006; VanTassel-Baska, Quek, & Feng, 2007).

Using a quasi-experimental design, 37 experimental classrooms implemented one William & Mary unit in Grades 3, 4, or 5. More rigorous assessment was employed in this study, including the investigator-developed TCT and the reading comprehension section of the *Iowa Test of Basic Skills* (ITBS), in addition to the performance-based measures used in earlier studies.

The longitudinal sample for this three-year study involved 2,771 students, with 52–54% students in the experimental group and 48–46% students in the comparison group across the three years. Formal training for teachers in the implementation of the units was conducted for four days during each year of the project. Data analyses featured the use of a multivariate repeated measures MANCOVAs to assess within- and between-group differences. Effect sizes were calculated for all groups when significant results were obtained. Results suggested that students in experimental classes showed significant and important educational gains in critical thinking with effect sizes at moderate range across the three-year intervention ($p < .05$). While comparison students also showed significant gains in critical thinking, significant differences favored the experimental group with small effect sizes. Students across all ability levels demonstrated gains, including typical learners, promising learners, advanced readers, and gifted students. On the Reading Comprehension subtest of the ITBS, both experimental and comparison students showed significant growth, attesting to the value of both the experimental and comparison curricula and supplemental reading involvement. Performance-based measures also yielded significant and educationally important results for the experimental students in all ability groups, suggesting that the experimental curriculum is effective with a broad range of diverse learners.

Use of the Units with Differing Ability Levels

A SUBANALYSIS EXAMINED the efficacy of the curriculum for students across different ability levels. In the curriculum-based assessment for literary analysis and interpretation, based on the 1999 NAEP reading assessment (Feng et al., 2005), advanced readers and promising learners ($N = 115$), and gifted students ($N = 28$), showed significant growth and moderate to high effect sizes (Cohen's $d = .57$ to $.73$). Effect sizes for typical learners ($N = 240$) were moderate ($d = .36$), as were effect sizes for special education students ($N = 20$) ($d = .48$), suggesting that all groups gained educationally from the intervention. In the area of persuasive writing, results were even stronger with the high readers/promising learners and gifted groups achieving large effect sizes (i.e., 1.1 and .92, respectively), using Cohen's *d*. Typical learners also showed large effect sizes from the intervention at 1.0, as did special education students at .8. A small subsample of students was analyzed longitudinally to document growth trends across the three-year study. Despite small sample sizes, within subject effects were significant with moderate effect sizes across three years for gifted, high readers, and typical learners.

A subanalysis by students' ability level was also conducted on the ITBS reading assessment outcomes. These results showed strong effect sizes for typical learners ($d = .72$), moderate for high readers/promising learners ($d = .47$), and moderate to small effects for gifted and special education students ($d = .33$ and $.23$, respectively). The results suggest that the William & Mary curriculum can produce significant and educationally important learning gains in reading comprehension for students of all ability levels, as assessed by a well-respected standardized group achievement measure.

In schools, we have found extensive evidence of the curriculum being institutionalized, with many constituent groups voicing strong support for its impact. Teachers remarked that the units helped students look for the big picture instead of just memorizing a great deal of isolated information, and that they promoted teacher learning as well. Several administrators noted that teachers have learned to be coaches, letting kids hit or miss the mark. Teachers noted that after using more than one unit, students began to demonstrate improvements in habits of mind, writing, and self-reflection skills, and ability to work cooperatively in groups.

Parent Perceptions

Parents cited the benefits of the units' carryover into the home. One parent noted: "When my child hears a speaker, he starts to critique what is being said and how things are interrelated." Another parent related: "This notion of having three lines of argumentation has now permeated our life. We wanted to go bowling and my son kept saying 'elaborate.'" Students agreed that the gifted materials keep their minds working, and one perceptive young man observed: "We get smarter as the units get harder."

Research Findings in Brief

- Students in Title I schools exposed to the language arts units showed significant learning gains annually in reading comprehension when compared to students who used a basal reader or teacher-created materials (Bracken, VanTassel-Baska, Brown, & Feng, 2007; VanTassel-Baska, Bracken, Feng, & Brown, 2008).
- Students exposed to the language arts units showed significant learning gains annually in critical thinking when compared to students who used a basal reader or teacher-created materials (Bracken et al., 2007; VanTassel-Baska et al., 2008).
- Gifted, learning-disabled, and typical learners all showed significant learning gains in critical thinking through persuasive writing (Hughes, 2000).
- Subanalyses suggest that student growth in critical thinking may be bounded by the characteristics of the learner, teacher skills in soliciting critical thinking behaviors, and fidelity of curriculum implementation (Bracken et al., 2007; Hughes, 2000; VanTassel-Baska et al., 2008).
- Students who were exposed to the language arts curriculum showed significant and educationally important gains in literary analysis (VanTassel-Baska, Zuo, Avery, & Little, 2002; VanTassel-Baska, Johnson, Hughes, & Boyce, 1996).
- Students who were exposed to the language arts curriculum showed significant and educationally important gains in persuasive writing (Bracken et al., 2007; Hughes, 2000; VanTassel-Baska et al., 2008; VanTassel-Baska et al., 1996; VanTassel-Baska et al., 2002).
- Teacher acceptance of curriculum materials impacts the extent to which curriculum elements are employed, how students are challenged, and continued curriculum use (VanTassel-Baska et al., 1996).
- Continued use of the language arts curriculum over a three-year period significantly enhanced students' literary analysis skills and persuasive writing competency (Feng et al., 2005).
- Academic achievement effects were significant for all groups of learners regardless of socioeconomic status, ability level, or ethnicity (Bracken et al., 2007; VanTassel-Baska et al., 2008; VanTassel-Baska et al., 1996; VanTassel-Baska et al., 2000; VanTassel-Baska et al., 2002).

Conclusion

The use of high-powered curriculum materials designed with the needs of high-ability learners and the new curriculum reform paradigm in mind appears to result in greater learning on dimensions important to both language arts educators and educators of high-ability learners.

Teacher Education

Professional Development for Teaching Language Arts

Understanding the research on teacher quality and expertise is essential to understanding intervention research in reading. Expert teachers must have specific, pedagogically relevant content expertise (Shulman, 1987), which includes knowledge of how best to explicate concepts, demonstrate methods (Leinhardt & Greeno, 1986), and correct students' theories and misconceptions (Gardner, 1991). Recent studies on teacher effectiveness substantiate the critical role of sound teaching practices, especially emphasis on higher order cognitive skills (Wenglingsky, 2000). Moreover, the professional development literature suggests that teachers will adopt new pedagogy if they believe it will enhance student learning (Kennedy, 1999). Thus, for meaningful and lasting instructional change to occur, teacher attitudes must first change relative to applications of new instructional techniques in the classroom (Guskey, 2000). The use of content-relevant pedagogy, delivered in a context of application and reflection, was found crucial to the transfer of professional development to practice (Guskey, 1994).

Application of Research on Teaching to William & Mary Professional Development Workshops

The William & Mary professional development workshops used to train teachers to implement these units call for a thorough understanding of relevant teaching models to be applied to the classroom. These models are introduced, practiced, and discussed in a debriefing period in segments of 45 minutes each. Teachers are encouraged to observe the use of models embedded in actual lesson plans and to discuss how they enable learners to progress in their learning to think about text critically and their own writing and presentations. A sample workshop outline features at least six teaching models across two days that provide teachers with the necessary scaffolding for teaching the units.

Training workshops sponsored through the Center for Gifted Education provide teachers with competency in implementing the core unit strategies as well as informal tips for teaching various strands in the unit.

For the past 23 years, the Center for Gifted Education has offered language arts curriculum institutes at The College of William & Mary and in-service workshops for teachers and administrators throughout the United States and the world. The language arts curriculum in-service programs were designed to enable participants to relate state language arts frameworks to national standards and to see the William & Mary Center for Gifted Education language arts units modeled on these standards, to select appropriate language arts materials for high-ability learners, to employ successful instructional strategies in language arts teaching, and to implement the language arts units in the classroom. To date, over 15,000 educators throughout the United States and at 18 international sites have participated in the institutes.

Based on these experiences, we recommend minimally a two-day training session for all teachers using the units. Workshops are generally comprised of these core segments:

1. Overview of language arts curriculum
2. Teaching concepts
3. Teaching the Paul Reasoning Model
4. Using Literature Webs, Vocabulary Webs, and Venn diagrams to analyze literature
5. Teaching persuasive writing
6. Using debate
7. Teaching research skills
8. Implementing a specific unit of study
9. Authentic assessment in the language arts classroom
10. Alignment with state standards

As a result of such curriculum development and teacher training efforts, the language arts units have been employed successfully over the past 23 years as a way of promoting the learning of high-ability and gifted students. They have provided an important catalyst for promoting the synergistic aspects of new learning principles as well as enhancing the elements of curriculum for these learners—one that is interdisciplinary, one that is challenging and engaging, and one that promotes generative work.

References

Alvermann, D., Young, J., Weaver, D., Hinchman, K., Moore, D., Phelps, S., et al. (1996). Middle and high school students' perceptions of how they experience text-based discussions: A multi-case study. *Reading Research Quarterly, 31,* 244–267.

Applebee, A. N., Langer, J. A., Nystrand, M., & Gamoran, A. (2003). Discussion-based approaches to developing understanding: Classroom instruction and student performance in middle and high school English. *American Educational Research Journal, 40*(3), 685–731.

Applebee, A., & Langer, J. (2006, April). *Partnership for Literacy: Abstract. The Partnership for Literacy: A study of professional development, instructional change, and student growth.* Presented at the annual convention of AERA, San Francisco, CA.

Baskin, B. H., & Harris, K. H. (1980). *Books for the gifted child.* NY: R. R. Bowker.

Boulineau, T., Fore, C., Hagan-Burke, S., Burke, M. (2004). Use of storymapping to increase the story-grammar text comprehension of elementary students with learning disabilities. *Learning Disability Quarterly,* 27, 105–121.

Brabham, E. G., & Villaume, S. K. (2001). Building walls of words. *The Reading Teacher, 54*(7), 700–702.

Bracken, B. A., VanTassel-Baska, J., Brown, E. F., & Feng, A. (2007). Project Athena: A tale of two studies. In J. VanTassel-Baska & T. Stambaugh (Eds.), *Overlooked gems: A national perspective on promising students of poverty* (pp. 63–67). Washington, DC: National Association for Gifted Education.

Chall, J. S. (2000). *The academic achievement challenge: What really works in the classroom?* NY: Guilford.

Chow, P., & Chou, C. (2000). Evaluating sustained silent reading in reading classes. *The Internet TESL Journal,* 6(11).

Daniels, H. (2002). *Literature circles: Voice and choice in book clubs & reading groups.* Portland, ME: Stenhouse Publishers.

Deshler, D. D., Schumaker, J. B., Lenz, B. K., Bulgren, J. A., Hock, M. F., Knight, J., et al. (2001). Ensuring content-area learning by secondary students with learning disabilities. *Learning Disabilities Research & Practice, 16,* 96–109.

Feng, A., VanTassel-Baska, J., Quek, C., Bai, W., & O'Neill, B. (2005). A longitudinal assessment of gifted students' learning using the integrated curriculum model: Impacts and perceptions of the William & Mary language arts and science curriculum. *Roeper Review, 27,* 78–83.

Fielding, L., & Pearson, P. (1994). Reading comprehension: What works. *Educational Leadership, 51*(5), 62–68.

Fuchs, D., & Fuchs, L. S. (2007). A model for implementing responsiveness to intervention. *Teaching Exceptional Children, 39,* 14–20.

Gardiner, S. (2001). Ten minutes a day for silent reading. *Educational Leadership, 9*(2), 32–5.

Gardner, H. (1991). *The unschooled mind: How children think and how schools should teach.* NY: Basic Books.

Gersten, R., Fuchs, L. S., Williams, J. P., & Baker, S. (2001). Teaching reading comprehension strategies to students with learning disabilities: A review of the research. *Review of Educational Research, 71,* 279–320.

Guskey, T. (1994). Results-oriented professional development: In search of an optimal mix of effective practices. *Journal of Staff Development, 15*(4), 42–50.

Guskey, T.R. (2000). Evaluating professional development. Thousand Oaks, CA: Corwin.

Hamel, F., & Smith, M. (1998). You can't play if you don't know the rules: Interpretive conventions and the teaching of literature to students in lower-track classes. *Reading and Writing Quarterly: Overcoming Learning Difficulties, 14*(4), 355–77.

Hughes, C.E. (2000). A comparative study of teaching critical thinking about persuasive writing to average, gifted, and students with learning disabilities. Unpublished dissertation, College of William & Mary, Williamsburg, VA.

Kennedy, M. (1999). Form and substance in mathematics and science professional development. *NISE Brief, 3*(2), 1–7.

Knapp, M. S., Adelman, N. E., Marder, C., McCollum, H., Needels, M. C., Padilla, C., Shields, P. M., Turnbull, B. J., & Zucker, A. A. (1995). *Teaching for meaning in high-poverty classrooms.* NY: Teachers College Press.

Langer, J. (2001). Beating the odds: Teaching middle and high school students to read and write well. *American Educational Research Journal, 38*(4), 837–80.

Leinhardt, G., & Greeno, J. G. (1986). The cognitive skill of teaching. *Journal of Education Psychology, 78,* 75–95.

Mahurt, S. F., Metacalfe, R. E., & Gwyther, M. A. (2007). *Building bridges from early to intermediate literacy: Grades 2–4.* Thousand Oaks, CA: Corwin Press.

Mellard, D. F., & Johnson, E. (2008). *RTI: A practitioner's guide to implementing response to intervention.* Thousand Oaks, CA: Corwin Press.

Miller-Lachmann, L. (1992). *Our family, our friends, our world: An annotated guide to significant multicultural books for children and teenagers.* New Providence, NJ: Bowker.

National Assessment Governing Board. (1992). *Reading framework for the 1992 national assessment of education progress.* Washington, DC: United States Department of Education.

National Assessment of Educational Progress. (2005). *Trends in academic progress: Three decades of student performance in Reading and Mathematics.* Washington, DC: United States Department of Education.

National Institute of Child Health and Human Development. (2000). *Teaching children to read: An evidence-based assessment of the scientific literature on reading and its implications for reading instruction.* Washington, DC: US Government Printing Office.

National Research Council. (1996). *National science education standards.* Washington, DC: National Academy Press.

Newman, F. M., Bryk, A. S., & Nagaoka, J. K. (2001). *Authentic intellectual work and standardized tests: Conflict or coexistence?* Chicago: Consortium on Chicago School Research.

Peak, J., & Dewalt, M. (1994). Reading achievement: Effects of computerized reading management and enrichment. *EPS Spectrum: Journal of School Research and Information, 12*(1), 31–34.

Pearson, P. D., & Gallagher, M. C. (1983). The instruction of reading comprehension. *Contemporary Educational Psychology, 8,* 317–344.

Phelps, S. (2005). *Ten years of research on adolescent literacy, 1994-2004: A review.* Naperville, IL: Learning Points Associates.

Rief, S. F., & Heimburge, J. A. (2007). *How to reach and teach all children through balanced literacy.* San Francisco: Jossey Bass.

Rosenshine, B., & Meister, C. (1994). Reciprocal teaching: A review of the research. *Review of Educational Research, 64,* 479–530.

Samuels, S. J., & Wu, Y. C. (2004). The effects of immediate feedback on reading achievement. Unpublished manuscript.

Schorzman, E. M., & Cheek, E. H. (2004). Structured strategy instruction: Investigating an intervention for improving sixth-graders' reading comprehension. *Reading Psychology, 25,* 37–60.

Shulman, L. S. (1987). Knowledge and teaching: Foundations of the new reform. *Harvard Educational Review, 19*(2), 4–14.

Snow, C. E., Burns, M. S., & Griffin, P. (Eds.). (1998). *Preventing reading difficulties in young children.* Washington, DC: National Academy Press.

Taylor, B. M., Pearson, P. D., Peterson, D. S., & Rodriguez, M. C. (2003). Reading growth in high-poverty classrooms: The influence of teacher practices that encourage cognitive engagement in literacy learning. *The Elementary School Journal, 104*(1), 3–30.

The Four Blocks literacy model: What is the four-blocks? (n.d.). Retrieved April 11, 2008, from http://www.wfu.edu/education/fourblocks/about_fourblocks.html

Tindal, G., & Nolet, V. (1995). Curriculum-based measurement in middle and high schools: Critical thinking skills in content areas. *Focus on Exceptional Children, 27*(7), 1–22.

VanTassel-Baska, J. (1986). Effective curriculum and instructional models for talented students. *Gifted Child Quarterly, 30,* 164–169.

VanTassel-Baska, J. (1992, October). Developing learner outcomes for gifted students. *ERIC Bulletin,* 2–5.

VanTassel-Baska, J. (1995). The development of talent through curriculum. *Roeper Review, 18,* 98–102.

VanTassel-Baska, J. (2003). Differentiating the language arts for high ability learners, K–8. *CEC ERIC Digest,* Arlington, VA.

VanTassel-Baska, J., Avery, L. D., Little, C. A., & Hughes, C. E. (2000). An evaluation of the implementation of curriculum innovation: The impact of William & Mary units on schools. *Journal for the Education of the Gifted, 23,* 244–272.

VanTassel-Baska, J., Bracken, B., Feng, A., & Brown, E. (2006). A longitudinal assessment of Athena teachers' instructional improvement. AERA session presentation, San Francisco, April, 2006.

VanTassel-Baska, J., Bracken, B., Feng, A., & Brown, E. (2009). A longitudinal assessment of Athena students' learning outcomes. *Journal for the Education of the Gifted.*

VanTassel-Baska, J., Bracken, B., Feng, A., & Brown, E. (2008). A longitudinal study of reading comprehension and reasoning ability of students in elementary Title I schools. Manuscript submitted for publication.

VanTassel-Baska, J., Feng, A., Brown, E., Bracken, B., Stambaugh, T., French, H., McGowan, S., Worley, B., Quek, C., & Bai, W. (2008). A study of differentiated instructional change over 3 years. *Gifted Child Quarterly, 52*(4), 297–312.

VanTassel-Baska, J., Johnson, D. T., Hughes, C. E., & Boyce, L. N. (1996). A study of language arts curriculum effectiveness with gifted learners. *Journal for the Education of the Gifted, 19,* 461–480.

VanTassel-Baska, J., Quek, C., & Feng, A. (2007). Developing structured observation scales for instructional improvements in classrooms accommodating gifted learners. *Roeper Review, 29,* 84–92.

VanTassel-Baska, J., & Stambaugh, T. (2006). Project Athena: A pathway to advanced literacy development for children of poverty. *Gifted Child Today, 29*(2), 58–65.

VanTassel-Baska, J., Tieso, C., & Stambaugh, T. (2007, November). *Project Athena: Longitudinal effects of a reading intervention curriculum on teachers and students.* Paper presented at the National Association for Gifted Children Annual Conference, Minneapolis, MN.

VanTassel-Baska, J., Zuo, L., Avery, L., & Little, C. (2002). A curriculum study of gifted-student learning in the language arts. *Gifted Child Quarterly, 26,* 30–43.

Villaume, S. K., & Brabham, E. G. (2002). Comprehension instruction: Beyond strategies. *The Reading Teacher, 55*(7), 672–676.

Vollands, S. R., Topping, K. J., & Evans, R. M. (1999). Computerized self-assessment of reading comprehension with accelerated reader: Action research. *Reading and Writing Quarterly, 15*(3), 197–211.

Wenglingsky, H. (2000). *How teaching matters.* Princeton, NJ: Educational Testing Service.

Wiesendose, K. D., & Baker, L. (1989). SSR: Its effects on students' reading habits after they complete the program. *Reading Horizons, 29*(3), 162–166.

Yoon, J. (2002). Three decades of sustained silent reading: A meta-analytic review of the effects of SSR on attitude toward reading. *Reading Improvement, 39*(4), 186–195.

Curriculum Framework

SECTION 2

The William & Mary Center for Gifted Education Curriculum Framework

The curriculum framework for developing the language arts units for high-ability learners is based on three major types of learner outcomes: concept outcomes organized around the theme of change, content outcomes organized around the strands of the language arts (literature, writing, oral communication, and language study), and process outcomes organized around the Elements of Reasoning.* Each set of outcomes guided the development of the units such that most lesson plans reflect an emphasis on each type of outcome. Figure 2-1 portrays this idea graphically.

The diagram on the following page (Figure 2-2) represents the relationship of learner outcomes and teaching strategies employed in the language arts framework and underlying units of study. The conceptual structure of learner outcomes outlined on the left provides the basis for the specific teaching strategies to be employed with students listed on the right. The units are centered on literature selections that provide the source for the conceptual outcomes to be explored and the catalyst for the learning strategies to be employed.

Figure 2-1: Emphasis of Learner Outcomes on Unit Development

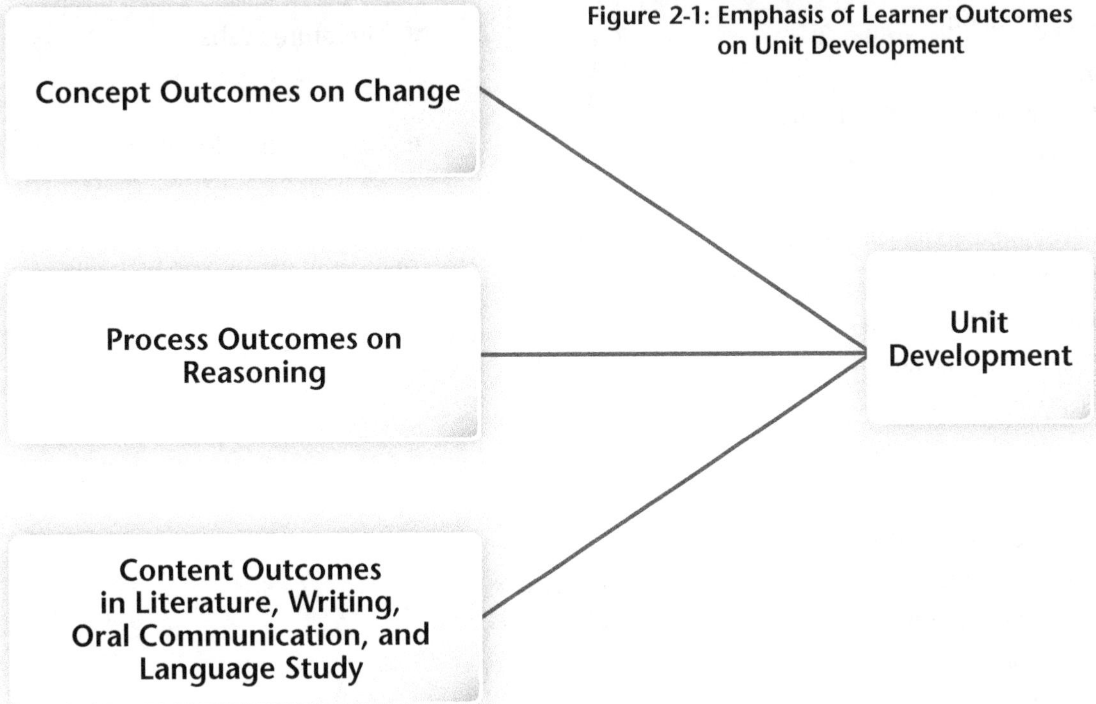

*Occasional variations in specific concept, process, or content focuses occur within the curriculum; see "Learner Outcomes" on pages 29–33 for more information.

Figure 2-2: Constructing Meaning Through Inquiry

What students need to understand

Change

1. Pervasive
2. Linked to time
3. Perceived as systematic or random
4. Represents growth and development or regression and decay
5. Occurs according to natural order or imposed by individuals or groups

Elements of Reasoning

1. Purpose, goal, end view
2. Issue of significance
3. Point of view
4. Assumptions
5. Concept mastery
6. Evidence
7. Inferences
8. Implications and consequences

Literature

1. Analysis
2. Interpretation

Writing

1. Developing a significant issue
2. Providing supportive evidence
3. Synthesizing a conclusion
4. Revising based on self-, peer, and teacher review

Speaking and Listening

1. Evaluative listening
2. Elements of persuasion
3. Argument formulation
4. Oral presentation

Linguistic Competency

1. Form of words
2. Function of words
3. Vocabulary
4. Usage

Active Interplay

Literature Selections

What teachers need to do with students

▼ Research projects

▼ Essays

▼ Written response logs

▼ Argument development

▼ Self-study grammar packets

▼ Higher level questions, using Elements of Reasoning

▼ Vocabulary Webs

▼ Literature Webs

▼ Concept development

Adapted from Novak, J. D., & Gowin, D. B. (1984). *Learning how to learn.* New York: Cambridge University Press.

Learner Outcomes: Concept Dimension

The concept of change was selected for development in the majority of language arts units based on its ease of application to various areas of the language arts as well as to other areas of study. Integral to understanding this concept is a set of generalizations derived from extensive reading on the concept in philosophy, sociology, and science. The generalizations related to the concept of change are:

- Change is pervasive.
- Change is linked to time.
- Change may be perceived as systematic or random.
- Change may represent growth and development or regression and decay.
- Change may occur according to natural order or be imposed by individuals or groups.

These generalizations have been converted into generic concept outcome statements for use in the units:

Students will be able to …

- √ Understand that change is pervasive.
- √ Illustrate the variability of change based on time.
- √ Categorize types of change, given several examples.
- √ Interpret change in selected works as progressive or regressive.
- √ Demonstrate the change process at work in a piece of literature.
- √ Analyze social and individual change in a given piece of literature.

Specific applications of these outcomes have been developed for the units of study:

1. The generalizations about change are used as one basis for literature discussion.
2. Vocabulary Webs encourage students to understand how words have changed over time.
3. Selected writing assignments address the concept.
4. Emphasis on the writing process, oral communication, and research illustrate the concept of change as a process of individual learning.
5. Metacognition is emphasized as a change strategy for learning.
6. Culminating unit experiences trace the concept of change across time periods, cultures, and pieces of literature.

While most units use this set of change generalizations as their focus, two units adopt different concept focuses: in *Utopia,* the concept of utopia is considered, while in *Patterns of Change,* cyclical changes are explored. All units employ the same concept development model focusing around a set of core generalizations.

Learner Outcomes: Content Dimension

Content outcomes based on the key strands in language arts have been developed for the units. Outcome statements have been derived from broad goals for reading/literature, writing, language study, and oral communication. These outcome statements frame important bases for teaching and learning in the unit. The goals and learner outcomes developed are listed here:

GOAL 1 ***To develop analytical and interpretive skills in literature.***

Students will be able to …

- √ Describe what a selected literary passage means.
- √ Cite similarities and differences in meaning among selected works of literature.
- √ Make inferences based on information in given passages.
- √ Create a title for a reading selection and provide a rationale to justify it.

Specific applications of these outcomes have been developed for the curriculum units:

1. Pre- and postassessments on literary analysis and interpretation are embedded in the unit.
2. Literature Webs and other graphic organizers are used to promote literature understanding and response.
3. Response journals and logs are used to link literature to writing in the immediacy of the classroom discussion.
4. Specific study of vocabulary and language embedded in key selections of literature enhances literary understanding.
5. Each selected literary piece is used in a shared inquiry model of discussion that focuses students' construction of meaning based on their reading.

GOAL 2 *To develop persuasive writing skills.*

Students will be able to …

√ Develop a written persuasive paragraph (thesis statement, supporting reasons, and conclusion), given a topic.

√ Complete various pieces of writing using a three-phase revision process based on peer review, teacher feedback, and self-evaluation.

Specific applications of these outcomes have been developed for the curriculum units:

1. Pre- and postassessments for writing using an argument model are embedded in the unit.
2. Students engage in the writing process approach.
3. Students develop at least one issue of significance and discuss it in written form.
4. Students use Concept Webs to organize their thinking prior to writing.
5. Assessment of written work includes peer, self-, and teacher evaluation.

GOAL 3 *To develop linguistic competency.*

Students will be able to …

√ Develop vocabulary power commensurate with reading.

√ Apply standard English usage in written and oral contexts.

√ Evaluate effective use of words, sentences, and paragraphs in context.

Specific applications of these outcomes have been developed for the curriculum units:

1. Vocabulary Webs are used to study the etymology, meaning, and relationships between words in literature. The webs promote increased word power and facilitate vocabulary analysis.
2. Revision and editing of written work give students opportunities to demonstrate and refine effective use of language.
3. Self-assessment and peer-assessment instruments provide opportunities to evaluate the use of language, vocabulary, and grammar.

GOAL 4 *To develop listening/oral communication skills.*

Students will be able to …

√ Organize oral presentations.

√ Evaluate an oral presentation, given a rubric with specific criteria.

Specific applications of these outcomes have been developed for the curriculum units:

1. The inquiry-based discussion model promotes active listening and expression of ideas.
2. Opportunities for oral presentations enhance communication skills.
3. Critical listening experiences are provided through guest and peer presentations.
4. Self-assessment and peer-assessment instruments provide opportunities to evaluate oral communication and elements of persuasion.

The unit intended for the youngest learners, *Beyond Words,* has slightly modified content goals; in lieu of the listening/oral communication goal is a goal relating to the identification, analysis, and use of figurative language.

Learner Outcomes: Process Dimension

JUST AS THE units promote a conceptual orientation in the teaching of language arts, they also emphasize a strong process orientation toward thinking and reasoning. Based on work in teaching critical thinking (Paul, 1992), the units focus on selected Elements of Reasoning for the teaching of reading, writing, speaking, and listening skills. Virtually all modes of communication involve these elements. Table 2-1 illustrates the Elements of Reasoning, with specific applications and assessment criteria related to the language arts curriculum.

Table 2-1

Elements of Reasoning	Application Questions	Criteria for Assessment
1. Purpose, goal, or end view (e.g., does the student have a purpose—is it stated orally or in writing?)	What is the author's purpose in __________? What is the purpose of your essay (speech)?	Clarity, significance, realism, and consistency
2. Issue of significance, question at issue, or problem to be solved (e.g., can the student frame an issue—in writing, in debating, etc.?)	What is the central problem for the characters in the story? What is the major issue at stake?	Clarity in problem/issue formulation
3. Point of view (e.g., can a student formulate a consistent point of view and represent multiple points of view fairly?)	What is the author's point of view? What is your perspective on __________? Why?	Clarity and consistency (broad, flexible, fair)
4. Assumptions (e.g., can a student articulate the assumptions behind his or her reasoning?)	Why do you react to the story in that way? What role do values and beliefs play in your perspective?	Clarity, justification, importance, consistency
5. Concept mastery (e.g., can students recognize underlying principles and concepts in an argument or text?)	How does the concept of __________ contribute to your understanding of story elements?	Depth, clarity, relevance
6. Evidence (e.g., can students present data to support a claim/issue/idea that they express in written or oral form?)	What are the reasons for your point of view? Why do you think __________ is better than __________? Provide evidence.	Relevance, adequacy, consistency
7. Inferences (e.g., can students draw accurate inferences from what they read, write, say, or hear?)	What inference do you draw from the author's ending about what happens to __________? What is your conclusion to the essay?	Relevance, adequacy, consistency
8. Implications and consequences (e.g., can students make valid implications from ideas and data provided to them?)	What plan of action could be developed based on your reading of the textbook censorship issue?	Significance, realism

Although these Elements of Reasoning are not directly assessed in the unit, they are applied in the teaching of all the language arts through several approaches:

- Each question cluster for discussion uses the key Elements of Reasoning as a backdrop.
- The Research Model is patterned on the Reasoning Model.
- The argument model promoted in writing assignments stresses the elements of purpose, evidence, and conclusions.
- Oral presentations observed and presented by students are organized and critiqued using selected Elements of Reasoning.
- Listening activities call for students to identify speaker purpose, evidence for ideas, and conclusion.

The *Beyond Words* unit takes a slightly modified approach in its process dimension, focusing on analogical reasoning, with the desired outcomes of solving verbal analogy problems, using analogies as support for understanding new words, and analyzing figurative language that appears in analogy form.

Summary

The overall goals of the units are listed according to content, process, and concept emphases. Within the units, alignment charts are presented in the Unit Planner and at the beginning of each lesson to demonstrate the connections of the goals to individual lessons.

Content Goals:

Goal 1: To develop analytical and interpretive skills in literature.

Goal 2: To develop persuasive writing skills.

Goal 3: To develop linguistic competency.

Goal 4: To develop listening/oral communication skills.

Process Goal:

Goal 5: To develop reasoning skills.

Concept Goal:

Goal 6: To develop an understanding of the concept of change.

Assessment

ASSESSMENT OF HOW a curriculum for high-ability students impacts learners is one of the most important aspects of all curriculum design work. It is at this level of analysis that one can begin to understand the learner's level of comprehension and knowledge of what we had hoped to teach. It is at this stage that we have a sense of "learning receptivity," rather than "social receptivity," in the learner. The purpose of the assessment process is really multidimensional. It provides insights into student progress in a curriculum and pinpoints future needs in a curricular area for a learner. As such, it is a critical tool for ongoing curricular planning. Moreover, assessment data instruct us about how well our deliberate planning and teaching of learner outcomes has fared. Under ideal circumstances, each stated learner outcome in a curriculum for the gifted will have a corresponding assessment technique so that each learning focus can be measured and evaluated.

Because the emphasis of our educational enterprise with the gifted is often different from that with typical learners with respect to contact time, delivery models, and learning levels, the match between learner outcomes and assessment approaches is crucial. Standardized tests normed on typical populations tell us almost nothing about growth in learning for gifted populations unless they are used off-level.

Principles in Developing an Assessment Model for Gifted Learners

WHAT, THEN, ARE appropriate assessment issues to consider in evaluating language arts interventions with the gifted? Generally, it is important to apply the following principles when building an assessment model for gifted students:

1. The assessment model should use multiple measures and varied types of measures. Some of the most promising approaches include portfolios of students' work, product evaluation, and observational checklists of student behaviors.
2. The assessment model should incorporate long-term and short-term measures. One interpretation of this idea is very familiar to most teachers. It suggests that the combination of frequent quizzes and less frequent tests is a more desirable approach to student assessment of learning than only one or the other. This idea has salience for other types of evaluative tools, as well. The use of short-term products combined with one long-term project is more revealing of what has been learned than only short-term projects or only one long-term project. This combination honors the concept of time series as a mode of assessment; we want to know how the learner has progressed incrementally, as well as where he or she has ended at the end of 32 weeks of intervention.
3. The assessment model should incorporate multiple approaches to assessing learning. A good combination might be pre–post, time-series, and product assessment. Because gifted learner outcomes are geared to higher levels than typical student outcomes, it becomes problematic to rely on only one approach to measure the outcomes desired. Moreover, gifted curriculum outcomes are frequently incompatible with the use of one design. Thus, a combination approach is recommended.

Assessment in the William & Mary units is ongoing and comprised of multiple options. Pre- and posttests assess student growth in literature and persuasive writing. These serve multiple purposes. Performance on the preassessments establishes a baseline against which performance on the postassessment may be compared. In addition, teachers may use information obtained from the preassessments as an aid to instructional planning as strengths and weaknesses of individual students become apparent.

The development of performance-based assessments for the units was based on a careful study of several sources, including the National Assessment of Educational Progress 1990 Portfolio Study (National Center for Educational Statistics, 1992) and the Reading Framework (National Assessment Governing Board, 1992). The assessment approaches developed for the units were intended to span the language arts strands and the designated grade levels from 1 to 12. The literature selections and writing prompts are tailored to each unit of study. Authentic means of performance assessment were developed and incorporated for each strand, with the activities serving both as assessments and learning experiences.

The purposes of the performance-based assessment approach used in the units are as follows:

- **To assess learner outcomes of significance in the classroom:** By comparing pre/post results in a unit of study, teachers can understand how much high-ability students have grown in the particular dimension of the curriculum under study. Such data also provide a deeper insight into areas of growth still needed.
- **To derive important data for planning appropriate instruction (preassessment function):** Preassessment allows teachers to see where students are functioning in respect to a particular type of task demand. For example, who can find ideas in unfamiliar text and who cannot? These data should be used to target specific teaching toward students needing it in some aspect of the language arts, based on preassessment results.
- **To determine needed emphases in the instructional process:** The performance assessments provide data for teachers to decide what aspects of instruction need more attention. For example, if students can't elaborate appropriately, a lesson on "how to elaborate in written form" might be developed.

Teachers are encouraged to use the assessments in a dynamic way to enhance overall instruction. The assessments should therefore be treated as a part of the instructional package and should be discussed and used for instruction immediately after students have completed them.

Literature

PREASSESSMENT IS BASED on the first literature selection of each unit; postassessment is based on the last literature selection for each unit. Each piece of literature was carefully selected to be tailored to the unit's focus and the developmental level of the students. Regardless of the selection, each student is asked to respond to specific aspects of the reading.

The questions are intended to probe the student's ability to derive meaning from a piece of literature. The first question looks at a global notion of meaning (main idea), while the second focuses on a specific sentence in which some inference and interpretation are required. The third item not only explores the student's ability to make inferences but also reaches into the concept dimension of learner outcomes to evaluate a student's identification and interpretation of the concept of change (with the exception of *Utopia*) in a piece of literature. The fourth item concentrates the student's attention on synthesis of important text elements into an appropriate title.

Writing

A PROMPT FOR a persuasive essay is provided with the first and last literature pieces for each unit. Students are asked to respond to an issue in a paragraph structured as follows:

1. Statement of a point of view regarding whether the selection should be required reading for the student's grade level.
2. List of three reasons to support the given point of view, with elaboration.
3. Conclusion to the argument.

In scoring the writing assessment, emphasis is placed on evaluating the quality of the student's arguments rather than on mechanics. We also encourage teachers to teach the writing rubric to students so that they can effectively use it for peer and self-assessments. The use of the writing assessment model then involves multiple steps:

1. Administer the preassessment.
2. Discuss preassessment piece.
3. Teach the Hamburger Model of Persuasive Writing as a device to encourage student internalization of persuasive essay development.
4. Provide multiple exemplary pieces of persuasive writing for student analysis.
5. Provide students practice in developing "hamburger" paragraphs and multiparagraph essays.
6. Teach the persuasive writing rubric to students, giving them a practice essay to score and discuss. Use student exemplars provided in the units to discuss strong, mediocre, and weak responses to a particular prompt.
7. Engage students in peer and self-assessment of persuasive writing on an ongoing basis.
8. Administer the postassessment for persuasive writing. Discuss prompt with students.

Additional work in other writing forms may be found throughout the units. Approaches to assessing these writing tasks are included with the relevant lessons. They include self-, peer, and teacher assessment forms that allow for multiple perspectives to coalesce using the same criteria for student performance.

Portfolio assessment techniques are encouraged for assignments in which the teacher implements the full writing process. Thus, the portfolio might contain a student's prewriting sample, first draft, second draft, edited draft, and final proofed copy.

Other Assessment Tools

Teachers may find specific assessment tools with individual lessons. These include protocols for evaluating oral presentations, the unit research project, and a final written assessment on how well students understand the unit's overarching concept. These assessments may be useful in ascertaining student growth in other relevant dimensions of the language arts framework.

Teachers are encouraged to use the following to reinforce and augment the formal assessments employed in the units:

- *Response Journal:* Each student may use a spiral notebook or composition notebook as a Response Journal. As part of a reaction to each literature selection, the student writes a response to a question that is posed about that piece of literature. The teacher is encouraged to read the journal and write comments to the student.
- *Writing Portfolio:* Each student may maintain a manila folder as a writing portfolio. In it, all formal writing assignments are arranged chronologically. At the conclusion of each writing assignment, students may be asked to prepare writing self-assessments in which they reflect upon their work as writers.
- *Student–Teacher Conferences:* Opportunities should be provided for each student to meet periodically with the teacher to discuss current work and plans for further development.

Although assessment is not always specified for lesson activities, it is assumed that the teacher of the units will employ the instruments provided in the lessons in assessing ongoing activities and products. Pre- and postassessment instruments appear in the lessons in which they are to be administered and then used for instructional purposes.

References

National Assessment Governing Board. (1992). *Reading framework for the 1992 National Assessment of Educational Progress.* Washington, DC: U.S. Government Printing Office.

National Center for Education Statistics. (1992). *National assessment of educational progress's 1990 portfolio study.* Washington, DC: U.S. Department of Education.

Novak, J. D., & Gowin, D. B. (1984). *Learning how to learn.* NY: Cambridge University Press.

Paul, R. (1992). *Critical thinking: What every person needs to survive in a rapidly changing world.* Sonoma, CA: The Foundation for Critical Thinking.

References

National [illegible] (1992). [illegible] Washington [illegible]

[illegible]

[illegible]

[illegible]

Instructional Support for Special Needs Learners

SECTION 3

Special needs learners, including English Language Learners (ELL) and twice-exceptional learners, may benefit from using the William & Mary language arts units. Understanding what works with these populations and making adaptations and accommodations is critical to effective implementation.

Working with English Language Learners (ELL) in the William & Mary Units

Research on working successfully with ELL students in the language arts classroom involves attention to various approaches that are consonant with the William & Mary units. There is a strong emphasis in the units on the use of visuals, the use of scaffolds for instruction, and a multifaceted vocabulary development process. All lessons use constructivist models for instruction.

ELL students benefit from a combination of approaches that involve constructivist pedagogy, including strategy-based instruction, scaffolding, and metacognition. Strategy-based instruction refers to classroom procedures where the teacher incorporates language learning strategies in language teaching. Higher proficiency students are more likely to use learning strategies than their lower-proficiency counterparts. Explicit instruction, the teaching of learning strategies, coupled with application of those strategies in a subject-area discipline, greatly enhance student learning. Scaffolding or guided support is helpful in that it provides a situation where a knowledgeable participant can create supportive conditions in which the novice can participate, and extend his or her current skills and knowledge to higher levels of competence (Pawan, 2008). Metacognition can enhance learning efficiency and self-efficacy. Through a four-step process (choice of a text at an appropriate difficulty level, selection of strategies for instruction, structuring of lessons and the writing of transcripts for guiding the presentation of strategies, the adaptation of instruction to suit learner needs and reactions), ELL students can learn how to read effectively (Zhang, 2007). One study suggested that ELLs who critically analyze text even before they have mastered English are less likely to be bored in school (Daniel, 2008).

When planning instruction for ELLs, culturally responsive teachers identify language and content objectives, including whether the ELLs will be asked to understand aural input, to speak to the teacher and classmates, or to read and write. When planning lessons, teachers consider how these students critically analyze, interpret, discuss, and internalize new information (Daniel, 2008).

Vocabulary gains for ELL students were found in both narrow reading activities and reading plus vocabulary-focused activities. Enhanced reading conditions led to more gains in vocabulary acquisition. It was also confirmed that narrow reading can greatly enhance formal knowledge (Min, 2008). Lessons should include additional activities such as asking pupils in small groups to use the new vocabulary items to create short stories. The teacher can include nontext documents (newspapers) and have learners engage in word-search activities and have students use words in a sentence to reflect meaning (Ajayi, 2005).

Activities where students can work together in playful atmospheres create greater opportunities for language learners and language proficient learners to learn together (Ajayi, 2005). Vocabulary instruction should allow for a multiplicity of activities that can potentially offer learners more possibilities in activity choice and the manner to engage them (Ajayi, 2005).

For students who are just beginning to learn English, reading lessons that are shorter and more frequent may prove most effective (Helman & Burns, 2008). These mini lessons should do the following:

- Provide visual support for new words through pictures, objects, or actions.
- Give students opportunities to hear new words in context and ask questions about what they mean.
- Connect the oral and written forms of new reading words.
- Have students use new words in their own sentences.
- Encourage students to self-monitor for understanding of word meaning, such as sorting words they can read into "I know what it means" and "I don't know what it means" (Helman & Burns, 2008).

These lessons may be placed in a language arts center in the classroom. Second language learners must have access to comprehensible input that is just beyond their current level of competence, and they must have opportunities to produce output for meaningful purposes. Social interaction in which ELLs actively participate fosters the development of conversational and academic English. Explicit attention to linguistic form and function facilitates second language learning. When the lesson is too demanding for ELLs, extra linguistic supports give them a medium other than language through which to access the content, such as visuals. Giving clear and explicit instructions also aids ELL students in understanding how to function successfully in language arts classrooms (Lucas, Villegas, & Freedson-Gonzalez, 2008).

Working with Twice-Exceptional Learners in the William & Mary Units

Gifted students with learning disabilities, attention deficit/hyperactivity disorder (ADHD), and visual impairments demonstrate a discrepancy in tested potential and school performance, as well as discrepancies between verbal and nonverbal subsections on ability tests such as the WISC-R. School performance is often average.

Children with special needs resulting from their high abilities and their learning problems are often poorly served in school (Karnes, Shaunessy, & Bisland, 2004). Often educators' first impressions lead them to classify such a child as having below-average ability versus having a learning disability, and certainly not as possessing a gift. Students may receive content remediation instead of compensatory strategies, and high-potential students with special needs are likely to underachieve (Reis, McGuire, & Neu, 2004). Intervention focuses more on remediation of difficulties and less on the development of strengths and talents (Reis & McCoach, 2002). Another problem that results from misdiagnosis is harmful intervention. For example, the behaviors of ADHD and giftedness are often the same, frequently causing an intervention that "medicates the giftedness" right out of the child (Baum & Olenchak, 2002).

Students with learning disabilities possess unique characteristics of persistence and individual interests. They also show lower self-efficacy than peers without diagnoses. Highly successful adults with learning disabilities stress the importance of persistence, self-confidence, the will to conquer adversity, and strong character. Remediation of basic skills has been proven ineffective; rather, development of compensatory strategies (study strategies, note-taking skills, time management, test-taking, cognitive strategies, compensatory supports, and environmental accommodations) to perform a task have all been more successful (Baum & Owen, 1998) All students contributed their success in college to the use of compensatory strategies, lighter course load, special programs for learning disabled (LD) students, and the use of types of equipment (Reis, McGuire, & Neu, 2000). The creation of a personal plan for academic success varied among participants but always included the use of carefully selected and individually necessary compensation strategies (Reis et al., 2000).

Twice-exceptional students may experience increased frustration resulting from heightened expectations and higher standards for achievement that go along with being gifted. Many twice-exceptional students develop low self-concepts after starting school and have difficulty with social skills (King, 2005). Disabilities may lower IQ scores dramatically such that these students may not qualify as gifted. Behavior at home may be far different than at school (Besnoy, Manning, & Frances, 2005). Students with LD are less likely to be leaders, less likely to be popular, and are rejected more often.

Instructional Variables That Can Facilitate Success for Twice-Exceptional Students

Twice-exceptional learners may require special accommodations to help them succeed in using the William & Mary units. The amount of time required for success will vary depending on the task and topic. Students may need time for additional practice while others are working. The structure of the curriculum should be organized conceptually. Pedagogical structure should use graphic organizers. The structure of classrooms should employ differentiated instruction, physical areas for quiet reflection, and small-group discussion. These students require emotional support, external scaffolding, and advocacy while keeping the complexity level high (Coleman, 2005). Type III instructional intervention offers a systematic approach that requires critical and creative thinking to solve problems and can produce high-quality responses and products (Newman, Zupko, & Newman, 2006).

Successful strategies for twice-exceptional students typically include: providing visual and tactile-kinesthetic formats; teaching content by teaching concepts first and details second; learning how to set realistic short-term goals and to take credit for reaching these goals; providing specific instruction in organizational techniques; allowing students to take tests in separate, supervised environments so they can either read the test aloud to themselves or have someone else read it to them; and using preassessments (Winebrenner, 2003).

Accommodations

Specific accommodations found helpful for special needs learners in these units of study include:

Cognitive Development

The teacher:

- Taps different learning modalities, such as auditory, visual, and kinesthetic.
- Uses vocabulary study techniques.
- Encourages the use and creation of word analogies.
- Employs expressive activities, role-playing, debate, and oral interpretation of written material.
- Employs puzzles, games, and spatial reasoning techniques.
- Uses challenging problems where students don't know algorithms to stimulate thinking.

- Employs creative thinking strategies such as brainstorming, synectics, and elaboration.
- Engages students in activities that employ inductive and deductive thinking.
- Integrates the arts into teaching.
- Uses concept webs and other learning scaffolds.
- Uses interdisciplinary approaches.
- Integrates technology.
- Asks students to reflect on their own learning in a variety of ways, such as through journals, classroom discussions, etc.
- Encourages exploring multiple perspectives.
- Uses biographies and autobiographies to provide role models of success.

Social-Emotional Development

The teacher:

- Provides personal encouragement that is based on performance level to each learner.
- Promotes individual student understanding of own giftedness.
- Communicates regularly with parents.

Written Expression Accommodations

The teacher:

- Breaks assignments down into smaller, manageable parts.
- Allows additional time.
- Reduces or alters written requirements.
- Has students proofread for one type of error at a time.
- Has students use scientific and technological products to communicate knowledge.
- Permits dictated response to a person or audio recorder.
- Uses prewriting strategies, including brainstorming, making a web, and drawing about the topic.

Organizational Accommodations

The teacher:

- Lists and verbally reviews step-by-step directions for assignments.
- Posts class and homework assignments in the same area each day and ensures that students record and/or have a printed copy.
- Verbally reviews class and homework assignments.
- Works with students to establish specific due dates for short assignments and time frames for long-term assignments.
- Breaks up tasks into workable and attainable steps.
- Provides examples and specific steps to accomplish tasks.
- Provides checkpoints for long-term assignments and monitors progress frequently.
- Has students review and summarize important information and directions.
- Coaches students about asking questions regarding unclear directions and assignments.

Specific accommodations for twice-exceptional students may include the use of the following:

- Removing distractions (seating, use of desk clocks).
- Providing cueing.
- Allowing classroom movement.
- Providing regular contact with parents.
- Providing visual, auditory, and written reminders of assignments, procedures, and tasks.
- Adjusting deadlines/time requirements for tests, homework, and special projects.
- Allowing for alternative assignments.

The William & Mary language arts curriculum also lends itself well to the use of bibliotherapy or videotherapy, where books and films are used to help students identify with a protagonist's problem. The use of such tools and instructional techniques such as discussions allows twice-exceptional students to talk about their concerns and vicariously gain insight into their own problems. Group discussions can be organized in small groups of three to five across multiple sessions (six to eight) to provide stability and the opportunity for growth in the process. A goal of bibliotherapy is to provide a way for twice-exceptional students to reflect on their own lives and problems at a safe distance, thus engendering a more reflective stance for their thinking about the future. The small group should ideally be comprised of all twice-exceptional students. If not, other gifted learners might be included who are special needs students as well, such as low-income and minority learners who can readily identify with the sense of alienation and frustration experienced in the school environment.

References

Ajayi, L. J. (2005). A sociocultural perspective: Language arts framework, vocabulary activities and English language learners in a second grade mixed classroom. *Journal of Instructional Psychology, 32,* 180–195.

Baum, S. M., & Olenchak, F. R. (2002). The alphabet children: GT, ADHD, and more. *Exceptionality, 10,* 77–91.

Baum, S. M., & Owen, S. V. (1998). High ability/learning disabled students: How are they different? *Gifted Child Quarterly, 32,* 321–326.

Besnoy, K. D., Manning, S. K., & Frances, A. (2005). Screening students with visual impairments for intellectual giftedness. *Review, 37*(3), 134–140.

Coleman, M. R. (2005). Academic strategies that work for gifted students with learning disabilities. *Teaching Exceptional Children, 38*(1), 23–32.

Daniel, M. C. (2008). Helping English language learners: Preparing teachers to promote critical thinking and language acquisition. *College Reading Association Yearbook, 29,* 123–132.

Helman, L. A., & Burns, M. K. (2008). What does oral language have to do with it? Helping young English-language learners acquire a sight word vocabulary. *The Reading Teacher, 62*(1), 14–19.

Karnes, F. A., Shaunessy, E., & Bisland, A. (2004). Gifted students with disabilities: Are we finding them? *Gifted Child Today, 27*(4), 16–21.

King, E. W. (2005). Addressing the social and emotional needs of twice-exceptional students. *Teaching Exceptional Children, 38*(1), 16–20.

Lucas, T., Villegas, A. M., & Freedson-Gonzalez, M. (2008). Linguistically responsive teacher education. *Journal of Teacher Education, 59*(4), 361–373.

Min, H. (2008). EFL vocabulary acquisition and retention: Reading plus vocabulary enhancement activities and narrow reading. *Language Learning, 58*(1), 73–115.

Newman, J. L., Zupko, S., & Newman, J. L. (2006). TALENT-ed and TYPE III: An effective learning strategy for gifted students who are learning disabled. *Teaching Exceptional Children Plus, 2*(5), 1.

Pawan, F. (2008). Content-area teachers and scaffolded instruction for English language learners. *Teaching and Teaching Education, 24,* 1450–1462.

Reis, S. M., & McCoach, D. B. (2002). Underachievement in gifted and talented students with special needs. *Exceptionality, 10,* 113–125.

Reis, S. M., McGuire, J. M., & Neu, T. W. (2000). Compensation strategies used by high-ability students with learning disabilities who succeed in college. *Gifted Child Quarterly, 44*(2), 123–134.

Zhang, L. J. (2007). Constructivist pedagogy in strategic reading instruction: Exploring pathways to learner development in the English as a second language (ESL) classroom. *Instructional Science, 36*(2), 89–116.

Support Structures for Successful Implementation

SECTION 4

TEACHERS IMPLEMENTING THESE language arts units need to feel that they have the support necessary to make their teaching successful. Several areas of support are critical to making unit implementation work smoothly.

Administrative Support

TEACHERS MUST FEEL that their principals support them in the implementation process. Ways for principals to show support include:

- Attending workshops on the units with teachers.
- Observing teachers in the classroom (See observation scale in this section.)
- Holding periodic conferences with teachers to discuss implementation.
- Conducting a monthly discussion group on unit implementation.

Materials Support

TEACHERS NEED TO know that they can purchase and procure necessary materials for optimal unit implementation. Materials necessary include multiple copies of novels, appropriate dictionaries, and related classroom resources. Ways for school districts to provide materials support include:

- Asking the school media specialist to order resource materials on a cost-sharing basis with other funding.
- Having a central office coordinator order and deliver materials.
- Having the principal and/or central office personnel process materials procurement.

Teacher-to-Teacher Support

MANY TEACHERS BENEFIT from having others in the same building to talk with about an innovation. Some ways this effort can be supported include:

- Holding teacher meetings to discuss curriculum implementation.
- Videotaping lessons for discussion.
- Having teachers observe each other and discuss what they saw.
- Developing a mentor teacher or cognitive coaching program to encourage instructional dialogue.

Monitoring Classroom Implementation

JUST AS IMPLEMENTATION ideas for a new curriculum are important to share with teachers, it is equally important to ensure that a system for monitoring language arts classrooms exists that documents the nature of the language arts learning occurring.

Fidelity of implementation specifically may be monitored by use of the following form, shown in Table 4-1, entitled "The William & Mary Treatment Fidelity Form," to ensure that teachers are using the William & Mary models effectively.

It is recommended that the Classroom Observation Scales-Revised (COS-R) form, shown in Table 4-2, be used by appropriate educational personnel to determine the extent of implementation occurring in the classrooms. Principals, language arts coordinators, and instructional leaders in schools may employ the form to assess the success of unit implementation and teacher use of differentiation strategies. Judgments about other important dimensions of implementation may be discerned by the use of the COS-R. This instrument addresses six dimensions of teaching that impact the effective use of differentiation strategies for the gifted. These categorical dimensions include: planning, accommodation of individual differences, critical thinking, creative thinking, problem solving, and research. Interrater reliability of the form has been established at .89. Validity and reliability of the form have been assessed at .95 and .92, respectively.

Table 4-1: The William & Mary Treatment Fidelity Form

Directions: The following observation scale addresses the fidelity of implementation in the William & Mary Language Arts units. After reaching consensus with your observation partner, please check the relevant category describing the teacher's implementation of key instructional models.

Lesson # ________

The teacher...	Effective	Somewhat Effective	Ineffective	N/A	Comments
Content					
1. Instructed/practiced literary analysis and interpretation (Literature Web).					
2. Instructed/practiced word analysis (Vocabulary Web).					
3. Instructed/practiced persuasive writing (Hamburger Model).					
4. Instructed/practiced grammar activities.					
5. Structured questions for discussion of readings.					
6. Enhanced oral communication.					
Process					
7. Instructed/practiced the Reasoning Model.					
8. Instructed/practiced the Research Model.					
Concept					
9. Instructed/practiced concept webbing.					
10. Emphasized "change" in instruction and assignments.					
11. Instructed/applied unit generalizations about change.					
12. Emphasized relevant concepts, themes, or ideas in instruction and assignments.					

Table 4-2: The William & Mary Classroom Observation Scales, Revised

Joyce VanTassel-Baska, Ed.D.
Bruce Bracken, Ph.D.
Linda Avery, Ph.D.
Dianne Drummond, M.Ed.
Jeanne Struck, Ph.D.
Tamra Stambaugh, M.Ed.
Annie Feng, Ed.D.

Directions: Please employ the following scale as you rate each of the checklist items. Rate each item according to how well the teacher characteristic or behavior was demonstrated during the observed instructional activity. Each item is judged on an individual, self-contained basis, regardless of its relationship to an overall set of behaviors relevant to the cluster heading.

3 = Effective	2 = Somewhat Effective	1 = Ineffective	N/O = Not Observed
The teacher evidenced careful planning and classroom flexibility in implementation of the behavior, eliciting many appropriate student responses. The teacher was clear and sustained focus on the purposes of learning.	The teacher evidenced some planning and/or classroom flexibility in implementation of the behavior, eliciting some appropriate student responses. The teacher was sometimes clear and focused on the purposes of learning.	The teacher evidenced little or no planning and/or classroom flexibility in implementation of the behavior, eliciting minimal appropriate student responses. The teacher was unclear and unfocused regarding the purpose of learning.	The listed behavior was not demonstrated during the time of the observation. (Note: There must be an obvious attempt made for the certain behavior to be rated "ineffective" instead of "not observed.")

General Teaching Behaviors				
Curriculum Planning and Delivery	**3**	**2**	**1**	**N/O**
The teacher...				
1. Set high expectations for student performance.				
2. Incorporated activities for students to apply new knowledge.				
3. Engaged students in planning, monitoring, or assessing their learning.				
4. Encouraged students to express their thoughts.				
5. Had students reflect on what they had learned.				
Comments:				

Differentiated Teaching Behaviors				
Accommodations for Individual Differences	**3**	**2**	**1**	**N/O**
The teacher...				
6. Provided opportunities for independent or group learning to promote depth in understanding content.				
7. Accommodated individual or subgroup differences (e.g., through individual conferencing, student or teacher choice in material selection and task assignments.)				
8. Encouraged multiple interpretations of events and situations.				
9. Allowed students to discover key ideas individually through structured activities and/or questions.				
Comments:				
Problem Solving	**3**	**2**	**1**	**N/O**
The teacher...				
10. Employed brainstorming techniques.				
11. Engaged students in problem identification and definition.				
12. Engaged students in solution-finding activities and comprehensive solution articulation.				
Comments:				
Critical Thinking Strategies	**3**	**2**	**1**	**N/O**
The teacher...				
13. Encouraged students to judge or evaluate situations, problems, or issues.				
14. Engaged students in comparing and contrasting ideas (e.g., analyze generated ideas).				
15. Provided opportunities for students to generalize from concrete data or information to the abstract.				
16. Encouraged student synthesis or summary of information within or across disciplines.				
Comments:				

Creative Thinking Strategies	3	2	1	N/O
The teacher...				
17. Solicited many diverse thoughts about issues or ideas.				
18. Engaged students in the exploration of diverse points of view to reframe ideas.				
19. Encouraged students to demonstrate open-mindedness and tolerance of imaginative, sometimes playful solutions to problems.				
20. Provided opportunities for students to develop and elaborate on their ideas.				
Comments:				

Research Strategies	3	2	1	N/O
(Note: It is atypical for these to be observed in one session. Some teachers, however, may use Items #21–25 within a single period to illustrate the full research process to students. Please note those observations in the comments section.)				
The teacher...				
21. Required students to gather evidence from multiple sources through research-based techniques (e.g., print, nonprint, Internet, self-investigation via surveys, interviews, etc.).				
22. Provided opportunities for students to analyze data and represent it in appropriate charts, graphs, or tables.				
23. Asked questions to assist students in making inferences from data and drawing conclusions.				
24. Encouraged students to determine implications and consequences of findings.				
25. Provided time for students to communicate research study findings to relevant audiences in a formal report and/or presentation.				
Comments:				

Additional Comments:

SECTION 5

Assessing the Appropriateness of Language Arts Curriculum for Your School District

Introduction and Rationale for Language Arts Curriculum Assessment

THE TASK OF assessing language arts curriculum for appropriateness becomes critical in the context of national reform. Several national organizations such as the International Reading Association and the National Council of Teachers of English have called for all language arts educators to make fundamental changes both in content and in processes emphasized in material. Changing the factual and didactic orientation of the current curriculum and the materials that reinforce it to meet these new goals will require changing the very structures and foundations of the curriculum itself: a change in paradigm.

Two challenges are presented to reviewers of curricula who accept the validity and necessity of the "new curriculum" model. The first is to find a way to rate current curricula that is fair to the intent of the publishers and authors while attending to the assumption that in order to be effective, language arts instruction will follow a significantly new form. Basal texts that may be evaluated as perfectly sound under the old paradigm may in fact look less promising when rated using "new" standards. Nevertheless, such a review provides part of the demonstration of where and how changes need to be made to meet the demands of the 21st century.

The second challenge is to find a new and appropriate set of standards for determining differentiation for high-ability students. The National Language Arts standards document outlines literacy processes that should be cultivated in all American students (National Council of Teachers of English and International Reading Association, 1996). This list, while new to the goals of most general education programs, looks very much like the list of goals that teachers of the gifted have had for their students for some time. If all students should learn how to analyze and interpret literature, write persuasively, think productively, conduct research, and communicate well, then what will the new set of standards for gifted students be?

A good core curriculum is an essential foundation to exemplary language arts instruction. Because of the interest in engaging students in language arts over time, it has become increasingly important to select or create curriculum that simultaneously achieves several goals:

- Delivers content that is substantive, technologically relevant, and essential to an understanding of the communication arts.
- Demonstrates practices and "habits of mind" to give students practice in the behavior and thinking of writers and how to be productive members of a literary community.
- Delivers content and processes in a context that excites and entices students without diminishing the value of the content or reducing the practice of teaching to games.

- Provides opportunity for students to make connections among the language arts areas of reading, writing, speaking, and listening, and between language arts and other areas of study.

While such a core curriculum emphasis is essential for all learners, differentiating for the high-ability learner requires responding to the interests and behaviors displayed by these learners. Thus, high-ability learners need advanced content earlier and at a more complex and abstract level than do other learners, even given the new standards model.

Because curriculum materials are considered so crucial to the enterprise of teaching, we believe that the following set of criteria will prove valuable to school districts making decisions about materials in language arts. The users of the criteria may be (1) curriculum developers, (2) district-based curriculum or textbook review committees, or (3) individual teachers interested in materials for classroom use. We hope the process conveys a reasonable approach to decision making about educational materials in language arts and that practitioners will find it helpful.

Overview of the Review Process

Our goals for curriculum review were: (1) to develop a comprehensive evaluation system that would provide a template for reviewing all language arts curriculum materials, and (2) to generate curriculum reviews that would enable consumers to match available curricula with their locally identified needs. In order to reach these goals, we sought to conduct the following activities:

- Develop criteria by which a curriculum can be evaluated against a standard of excellence.
- Develop comprehensive criteria that would assess curricula in three areas: curriculum design, exemplary language arts, and tailoring for special populations.
- Create a system that enables consumers to compare one set of materials to another.
- Provide a multifaceted review of curricula that couples a numerical rating system with the personal reactions and insights of the reviewers.
- Institute a collaborative review forum that incorporates the perspectives of a language arts specialist, curriculum development expert, and an expert in resource materials.

The review process illustrated in Figure 5-1 was designed as a collaborative endeavor that involved these varied specialists. The curriculum specialists' expertise included general curriculum development, specialized curriculum for gifted learners, and the areas of speech communication, writing, and the teaching of literature and reading. The reviewers' classroom experience ranged from preschool to graduate school. In addition, each of them had experience teaching gifted learners at the elementary level and developing curriculum. This group with primary review responsibility was supported by a consultant group of educators and scholars who provided information on current issues in language arts and state-of-the-art curriculum materials.

Developing Criteria

The development of criteria was the cornerstone of the entire review process. The review team worked together to identify significant criteria, define each criterion, and test the criteria on sample curriculum.

Identifying the criteria forced the team to consider the essential elements of curriculum, which coalesced into three categories:

1. *Curriculum features:* elements that enable teachers to plan, deliver, and assess instruction.
2. *Exemplary language arts:* elements of subject matter content and process.
3. *Special populations:* elements addressing the needs and concerns of high-ability learners.

Figure 5-1: Curriculum Review Process

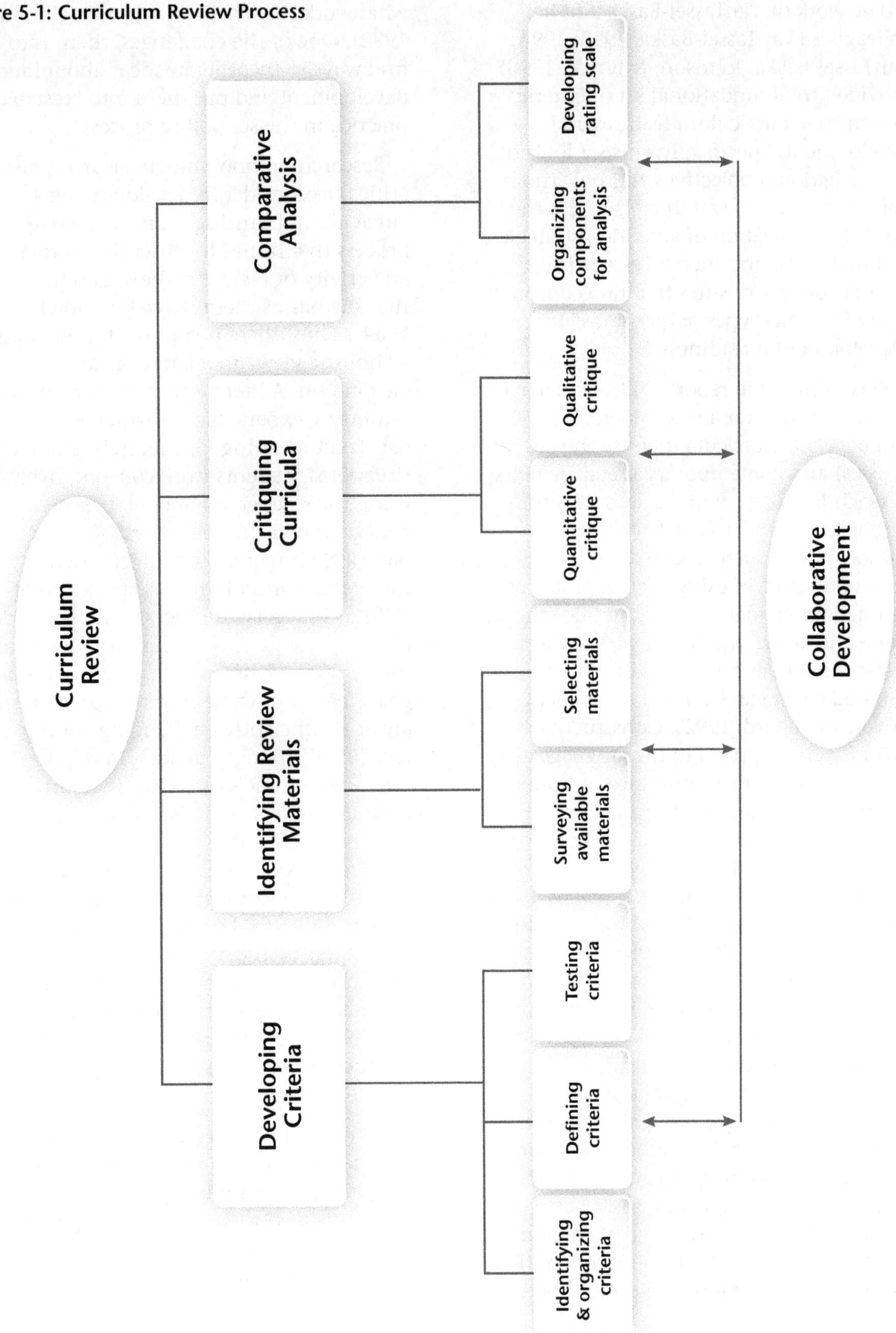

The work of VanTassel-Baska and her colleagues (VanTassel-Baska, 1992; 1994; VanTassel-Baska, Johnson, & Boyce, 1996) provided the foundational set of criteria for effective curriculum features and development. Specifically, this set looked at instructional objectives and how those objectives could be attained through the careful organization of activities, strategies, and materials, and then assessed. The criteria addressed issues that ranged from "use of various types of questions" to "developmental readiness."

Recent national reports in the language arts have called for a reconsideration of language arts curricula that use the best of classical and contemporary literature texts to teach language, writing, and literature through an inquiry-based approach (Suhor, 1984). Such reports also stress the importance of using such approaches throughout elementary and middle school. Close and active reading of various genres is also encouraged, even at the expense of broad coverage (National Assessment Governing Board, 1992). Constructivist theory, as it is applied to the language arts, has focused on the importance of students creating meaning from using literary sources, particularly in the writing process (Spivey, 1990). Other theorists view the province of teaching language arts as using the classical canon and teaching traditional forms of writing (Hirsch, 1987; Thompson, 1991). Accompanying modes of assessment have been developed that reflect intensive involvement with literary works, focusing more on the process of reading, the thought patterns of students engaged in it, and the power of thought brought to bear in connecting one work to another (National Assessment Governing Board, 1992). There exists, however, a significant gap between theory and practice. Researchers in literacy development generally have deplored the lack of curriculum research on testing what works in schools (Langer & Allington, 1992). One of the challenges, then, is to find ways to incorporate ideas about literacy development and put them into "testable" practice in the schooling process.

Research on how students learn is also critical to consider in developing new curriculum. Learning is an interactive process that brings together the learner, an activity or task, and the situation that surrounds them (Novak & Gowin, 1984). Thus, there is concern for ensuring a "holistic view" in a language arts curriculum. A literate environment provides rewarding experiences in which students construct meaning for themselves in real situations. Students work collaboratively, using the teacher as a model. Learners engage in revising their work as a welcome part of their regular school experience. An integrated curriculum uses communication skills as interrelated processes that support each other and as enabling skills across all subject areas. Outcome-based curriculum goals focus on whole thinking processes that are at a sufficiently challenging conceptual level. A "thinking" curriculum requires awareness of one's thinking, including attitudes, habits, and dispositions, as well as the critical and creative thinking processes about ideas. Such language arts curriculum encourages and supports student responsibility for learning and encourages and supports student choice, collaboration, and active participation. Such a curriculum also needs to be aligned so that what is written is also taught and tested, allowing instruction and assessment to become interrelated areas.

All of the new directions suggested by the theory and research of those in the language arts community tend to focus on some common themes for language arts curriculum reform in schools. These themes include the following:

- Making the learner the centerpiece for constructing meaning, using open-ended inquiry as a primary teaching tool.
- Integrating the language arts areas.
- Making connections to disciplines outside the language arts.
- Setting learner outcomes at high levels.
- Using authentic assessment.
- Developing in students the skills, attitudes, and dispositions of good readers, writers, and communicators.
- Using literature that satisfies both classical and multicultural considerations.

The special populations for whom specific criteria were developed included high-ability learners who were intellectually able and/or verbally talented. These criteria may be applied to the top 20 percent of the school age population. The work of VanTassel-Baska (1994) informed the criteria development for high-ability learners. The criteria emphasized acceleration and compression of content, higher order thinking in the language arts, creation of real products, and the exploration of meaningful themes and ideas.

After the criteria were identified, the review team worked together to define terms. Finally, the team tested the criteria by applying them to various curricula and comparing each team member's ratings. The tests and ensuing discussions led to new definitions and to revisions of criteria. In addition, team members located superior and inferior examples of various criteria; these examples then served as benchmarks for evaluating other curricula.

Why Schools Need to Review Language Arts Materials

In order for practitioners at all levels of education to make informed decisions about instruction, they must first become informed consumers. The model described here offers a way to examine current practices embedded in the materials we use in classrooms and to initiate change that is necessary for instructional improvement and educational reform.

The Review Process Enhances Decision Making

A collaborative review process is useful at all levels of instruction. At the classroom level, it enables teachers to make informed choices by providing the criteria to choose challenging materials for valid, worthy activities and the knowledge base to dismiss time-consuming distractions. At the school level, the collaborative review process provides principals and library media specialists with a vehicle for involving the entire staff in decision making on materials acquisitions. At the system and state level, it adds rigor to the textbook adoption process. The process provides an in-depth, systematic way to compare one curriculum with another, and it illuminates the lack of research base for many of the heavily marketed, commercial curricula.

The Review Process Facilitates Collaboration

The process of collaborative curriculum review offers an ongoing model to examine what is and is not working for curriculum delivery within a local school or within a school system. Once a group understands and internalizes a set of criteria, teachers and administrators have a method by which to improve instruction. In addition to defining terms and agreeing on standards, the process includes seeing another's perspective and tapping into another realm of expertise. The expertise within buildings, systems, and communities becomes available for meaningful, productive collaboration. Classroom teachers, subject specialists or experts in other fields, educators of special populations such as gifted learners and at-risk groups, guidance counselors and psychologists, and library media specialists all contribute different but essential knowledge and perspective. Collaborative review becomes a self-generating, learning process that results not just in a curriculum review but in a heightened awareness of possibilities for effective classroom practice.

The Review Process Is Dynamic

To be effective and viable, the review process and model require constant revisiting. For example, new research on the learning process and the consideration of evolving technology must continue to be incorporated into the criteria. In essence, continually revising criteria is part of an informed consumer process and essential to intellectual life. It is a fundamental aspect of education and one that teachers need to impart to students.

One of the values of this review process is that it considers curriculum resources other than textbooks. Tulley and Farr (1990) argued, "As long as educators continue to assume that the textbook is the curriculum, teachers will be powerless to exert change" (p. 169). The review process makes it evident that alternative materials such as modular curricula combine content and process in more powerful ways than reading-based textbooks. The need for change becomes urgently clear when choices are seen in a broader context, thereby expanding the range of possibilities.

Instructional improvement and the restructuring of schools depend on a shared vision of various groups and disciplines. Collaborative review offers a way for groups to identify mutual goals, to determine the criteria for excellence, and to work together. The implications of this review process for effective collaboration, combined with the possibilities for staff development and instructional improvement, warrant serious consideration.

Definitions of Criteria for Review

In the following section, the list of relevant criteria to consider in reviewing language arts curriculum materials is provided for all three phases of consideration. Each criterion is accompanied by a definition.

General Curriculum Features Evaluation Form: Phase I Review

Curriculum Design

1. **Rationale and Purpose**
   This feature addresses the reasons for developing a particular unit of study for use with a given group of learners at a particular stage of development. It provides the reader with a sense of the importance of the topic under study and why it is being taught.

   - **Substantive and worthy**
     Content is important and valuable; publishers/authors provide reasons why content was selected or the value is self-evident.
   - **Clear and understandable**
     Teachers can easily tell why the selected content is important. Rationale and purpose are written in meaningful and clear language rather than in educational jargon.
   - **Logical order and integrated structure to scope and sequence**
     The suggested order for presentation of topics and concepts makes sense both within a grade and from grade to grade.
   - **Identified outcomes consonant with purpose**
     The content and processes identified as desired goals of learning are consistent with the stated reasons to learn.

2. **Curriculum Content**
   This feature provides the scope of the unit in respect to content treatment and allows the reader to see the interrelationships of ideas that will guide the unit development process.

   - **Significant concepts**
     The language arts content is central to a fundamental understanding about a language arts content area and/or process.
   - **Significant information to explore concepts in depth**
     Enough factual information should be provided to cover selected concepts in depth, as opposed to a cursory sampling of information across many concepts.
   - **Topics support concepts**
     Individual areas of study in the curriculum illuminate/provide examples for larger, more abstract language arts concepts.
   - **Engaging style of presenting information**
     The material is attractive (well-illustrated, up-to-date, etc.), catches the learner's attention, and engages the learner.
   - **Topics and activities have personal meaning and social relevance for students**
     Information is presented from a child's point of reference.
   - **Allowance for curricular differentiation for gifted learners**
     The possibility to adjust content level or pace and acceleration of the curriculum exists. Suggestions for such adaptations are provided.

3. **Curriculum Responsiveness to Developmental Needs**
   This feature of the curriculum assures that there is an optimal match between the developmental readiness of the learner and the curricular expectations.

   - **Sequential exposure to language arts concepts from the concrete to the abstract**
     Depending on the age and/or grade level, the language arts ideas shift from being concrete with hands-on tasks and/or basic explanations to a more abstract and generalizable form.
   - **Active engagement with language arts materials used to support the curriculum**
     There are activities and resources available or suggested so that students can "do" language arts.
   - **Sequential use of visual materials from the pictocentric to the text-centered**
     Content is presented primarily through engaging and interesting picture books in early primary grades and moves to proportionately standard written text in higher grades.
   - **Identified outcomes consonant with purpose**
     The content and processes identified as desired goals of learning are consistent with the stated reasons to learn.

Classroom Design

4. **Instructional Objectives**
   This feature provides the focus and direction for learning in the unit. It specifies anticipated outcomes for students as a result of being taught a unit of study.

   - **Clear and understandable**
     A curriculum reader would know immediately what the students will be able to know and/or do as a result of a unit of study.
   - **Measurable**
     Techniques or suggestions are provided for teachers so they can tell whether or not students have achieved the learning outcomes.
   - **Related to overall rationale and purpose**
     The goals of an individual unit are consistent with the goals of the curriculum as a whole.

5. **Activities**
   This feature specifies what teachers will do to facilitate learning and what students will do to learn.

   - **Appropriate balance of teacher direction/student direction**
     Room is provided in the curriculum both to meet teacher goals and to allow for students to participate and contribute to the class.
   - **Developmentally appropriate activities**
     The activities take into account the level of cognitive, emotional, and physical development that is likely to be found in learners who will be doing these activities. Activities are challenging, yet achievable.
   - **Activities used to develop conceptual understanding**
     The activities allow students to deepen their understanding of core language arts concepts.
   - **Activities clarify, reinforce, and extend content**
     Activities serve a purpose related to learning content beyond repeating what students already know. They directly support the content-base of the unit.

- **Language arts integrated with other subjects**
  Interdisciplinary connections are presented. Activities encourage exploration of the relationships between language arts and other subjects such as social studies, science, math, art, and music.

6. **Instructional Strategies**
   This feature provides direction to readers around the major approaches to teaching that will be undertaken. It specifies teaching models, questioning techniques, and conferencing approaches used by the teacher.

   - **Varied strategies**
     Several different forms of instruction are suggested (e.g., inquiry activities, lecture, discussion, independent research).
   - **Opportunities for problem finding and solving**
     Students are encouraged to identify and solve problems that are not explicitly set out for them in advance.
   - **Opportunities for open inquiry**
     Projects that are issue-based or problem-based are open-ended with respect to the solution or the approach to the solution. Students are encouraged to formulate questions and explore possible answers to those questions.
   - **Varied grouping approach, (e.g., including opportunities for small group and independent work)**
     The curriculum suggests both large and small group activities and different ways these groups can be formed and used.
   - **Cooperative work focused on sharing multiple perspectives on issues**
     The process of sharing ideas is treated as more important than a single "right answer."
   - **Opportunities to practice decision-making strategies**
     Students are encouraged to make decisions rather than have the teachers tell them all procedures and outcomes.
   - **Use of various types of questions (e.g., convergent, divergent, evaluative)**
     There are a variety of questions suggested that stimulate different levels of thought, from knowledge through evaluation.

7. **Assessment Procedures**
   This feature specifies how students' learning in the unit will be assessed. It provides documentation for learning outcomes.

   - **Presence of pre- and postassessment measures**
     There are opportunities at both the beginning and the end of the unit to measure knowledge so that relative gain can be measured.
   - **Use of observational evaluation**
     Opportunities for assessment by observation are included.
   - **Use of authentic assessment**
     There are opportunities for students to demonstrate their skills and growth through authentic language arts tasks such as writing, discussion, and oral presentation rather than only through objective tests.

- **Objective attainment assessment measures**
  There are evaluation strategies that measure directly whether or not the student has met an objective.
- **Assessment based on ability to get and to use information**
  Assessment procedures require students to access and use information, rather than simply recognize facts.
- **Assessment based on outcomes of significance**
  The objectives that are assessed are valuable and important to language arts concepts, processes, or attitudes.
- **Opportunity for overall evaluation**
  Opportunity is provided for a holistic, integrated, final evaluation. There is some way of assessing whether objectives for a whole unit or curriculum have been achieved.

8. **Materials/Resources**
   This feature provides bibliographic references for use in implementing the unit. It includes both resources for teachers and materials for student use.

   - **Instructional materials begin with students' current knowledge**
     The materials provide for diagnostic assessment of knowledge and skills and/or introductory activities that encourage teacher assessment of knowledge levels.
   - **Supportive bibliography for teachers**
     Resources are suggested for teachers to enhance their knowledge of the subject.
   - **Frequent student misconceptions are identified for teachers**
     Teachers are alerted to what errors or pitfalls students commonly make or experience.
   - **Bibliography for student extension reading**
     Bibliographies are provided for the learners.
   - **Supportive handout materials (informational, worksheets, etc.)**
     Materials are included that are ready for duplication and that support the basic curriculum unit.

9. **Extension Ideas**
   This feature specifies follow-up learning opportunities for students that go beyond the prepared unit of study but are logical next activities, based on unit work. Suggestions for both group and independent work should be encouraged.

   - **Worthwhile, related activities for students to pursue independently**
     Meaningful suggestions are included for ways a student can extend the school learning experience to the home environment. Ideas, activities, and resources are suggested so the individual student can do extended work on a given topic, concept, or theme.

10. Technology Features*

This set of features specifies the extent to which the technology aspect of the curriculum is appropriate and effective in enhancing language arts learning experiences.

General

- Actively engages students in higher order thinking skills and activities
- Enhances and complements instruction
- Provides effective interaction
- Allows exploration otherwise prohibited by time or money
- Provides access to resources that are unavailable in print, timely, or more comprehensive than media center printed materials
- Contains several levels of difficulty
- Provides useful, corrective feedback
- Easy to use

Technical

- Uncluttered screen design
- Lucid, economical text
- Dynamic visuals for abstract concepts
- Useful help screens
- Effective self-pacing devices
- Comprehensive teacher manual that includes instructions for use and modification, inventory, and specifications

*This feature was not rated if the curriculum materials did not include it.

Exemplary Language Arts Features Evaluation Form: Phase II Review

1. **Reading/Literature**
    - **Choice of literature**
      The choice of literature or reading material is based on intellectual, affective, and multicultural considerations.
    - **Critical reading**
      The unit emphasizes expectations for critical reading behaviors.
    - **Textual analysis**
      The unit incorporates textual analysis of conceptually rich primary source material.
2. **Multiculturalism/Globalism**
    - **Quality of material**
      The unit incorporates the best of multicultural literature and related materials.
    - **Balanced perspective**
      There is a balanced perspective on at least three diverse cultures.
    - **Contributions of various cultural groups embedded**
      The contributions of various cultural groups are embedded rather than treated separately.
3. **Writing**
    - **Concept webbing**
      The materials use concept webbing as a way to organize ideas.
    - **Emphasis on different types of writing**
      The materials emphasize different kinds of writing, including descriptive, narrative, persuasive, expository, and technical.
    - **Use of writing strategies**
      The materials focus on strategies for developing a thesis statement, providing supportive evidence, and drafting a conclusion.
    - **Use of revision**
      The materials reflect the use of revision in the writing process.
    - **Use of workshop techniques**
      The materials reflect the use of workshop techniques (such as peer review and discussion of each other's writing).
4. **Language Study**
    - **Word relationships**
      The materials emphasize the development of word relationships, such as synonyms, antonyms, and analogies.
    - **Vocabulary development**
      The materials include opportunities to learn appropriate level advanced vocabulary.
    - **Linguistic competence**
      The materials encourage the development of linguistic competence in English, with an emphasis on grammatical structure.

- **History of language**
The materials include opportunities to learn about the history of language, etymology, and/or semantics.

- **Mechanics and usage**
The materials provide a review of basic mechanics needed to communicate, such as capitalization and punctuation.

5. Speaking/Listening Communication

- **Active engagement**
The materials provide opportunities for students to engage in active speaking and listening activities.

- **Opportunities for making oral presentations**
The materials provide opportunities for students to engage in various forms of oral expression, including dramatic presentations, persuasive speeches, and debate.

- **Causation**
The materials promote involvement of students responding to each other's presentations through questions, discussion, and critique.

- **Critical thinking**
The materials address critical thinking skills through listening and speaking.

6. Research Process

- **Provision of a model**
The students are directly taught a research model.

- **Issue/problem generation**
Alternatives are provided for students to develop their own issues.

- **Development of research questions**
Students are encouraged to participate in/develop researchable questions.

- **Broad-based communication**
Opportunities for research work that can be shared with multiple audiences are provided.

Tailoring for Special Populations Evaluation Form: Phase III Review

Differentiation for High-Ability Learners

1. **Provisions for acceleration and compression of content**
   Curriculum skills and concepts are organized on a continuum from "easy to difficult" concepts that would allow for easy teacher adaptation to students' individual instructional levels.
2. **Use of higher order thinking skills**
   The curriculum includes activities and questions that require learners to think at the levels of analyzing, evaluating, and creating (Bloom's Taxonomy Revised).
3. **Integration of content by key ideas, issues, and themes**
   The curriculum is organized according to broad-based concepts in language arts, such as change, patterns, and systems.
4. **Connection of ideas to other disciplines**
   The curriculum illustrates how language arts ideas have salience in other content areas such as music, art, social studies, and mathematics.
5. **Opportunities for advanced and broad-based reading**
   The curriculum provides students selected activities and materials that are sufficiently challenging and interdisciplinary for advanced learners.
6. **Use of multiple teaching resources**
   The curriculum encourages the use of multiple media, multiple readings, and multiple activities from other materials to teach skills and concepts.
7. **Use of diagnostic-prescriptive teaching**
   The curriculum provides an assessment approach that allows for pretesting and posttesting as well as ongoing assessment of learners' mastery of skills and concepts.
8. **Attention to instructional pacing**
   The teachers' guide notes that some learners can master the basic language arts content at a rate faster than other learners.
9. **Advanced reading level**
   The curriculum readability index is pitched at least one or two grade levels beyond the given designated level.
10. **Opportunities for students to develop advanced products**
    The curriculum provides suggestions for teachers to support student projects that involve original investigation.
11. **Opportunities for independent learning based on student ability and interest**
    The curriculum provides extension activities to be undertaken by students in various settings.
12. **Use of inquiry-based instructional techniques**
    The curriculum is based on a model of questioning that promotes the role of the student as investigator.

Procedures for Using the Curriculum Assessment Forms

1. Select a review team composed of teachers, administrators, and specialists with expertise in general curriculum, language arts curriculum, and curriculum for high-ability learners. Remember to include your library media specialist as a part of this group. A review team should not exceed six to eight individuals.
2. Read and review the Curriculum Assessment forms on pages 57–64 as a group, especially the review forms and the underlying definitions for the criteria presented in them.
3. Collect materials for team review.
4. Assign your most experienced reviewers to rate all three phases (no more than two individuals). Then assign each of the remaining reviewers the phase that corresponds best to their expertise. At least two reviews should be done for each individual phase.
5. Use the accompanying review forms found on pages 66–72 for this process.
6. Compile data across reviewers on the overall rating form and hold a team session to discuss reviews according to the specific material reviewed.
7. Make materials selection decisions based on (a) the match between the materials and the goals and objectives of your district language arts program, (b) the match with district needs for supplementary materials, and (c) the match with special population needs.

Curriculum Assessment Overall Rating Form

The Curriculum Assessment Overall Rating Form which follows provides a model for synthesizing the key features evaluated for each set of curriculum materials reviewed. The numerical average of reviewed ratings for each feature may be transferred onto this single sheet so that rating recommendations might be made according to individual features of the curriculum. For example, some curricula may be very strong in language arts and thus recommended for that feature. The same curricula may be found inadequate in general curriculum features and thus not recommended based on that set of criteria. The purpose and function of this rating form, then, is to provide a shorthand coding for the results of the multilayered review process.

The Curriculum Assessment Overall Rating Form

	Phase I: General Curriculum Features	Phase II: Exemplary Language Arts Features	Phase III: Tailoring for High-Ability Learners	Notes
Reviewer 1				
Reviewer 2				
Reviewer 3				
Reviewer 4				
Reviewer 5				
Reviewer 6				
Reviewer 7				
Reviewer 8				

The Curriculum Assessment Forms

General Curriculum Features: Phase I

Name of Reviewer: ______________________________

Title: ______________________________

Title of Curriculum to Be Reviewed: ______________________________

Appropriate Grade Level(s): ______________ Original Copyright Date: ______________

Date(s) of Revision: ______________________________

Directions:
Carefully read all curriculum materials and then rate the curriculum by each of the following criteria on a scale of: 5 = To an exemplary extent; 4 = To a good extent; 3 = Adequate; 2 = To a limited extent; and 1 = Not at all.

1. *Rationale and Purpose*

• Substantive and worthy	5	4	3	2	1
• Clear and understandable	5	4	3	2	1
• Logical order and integrated structure to scope and sequence	5	4	3	2	1
• Identified outcomes consonant with purpose	5	4	3	2	1

2. *Curriculum Content*

• Significant concepts	5	4	3	2	1
• Significant information to explore concepts in depth	5	4	3	2	1
• Topics support concepts	5	4	3	2	1
• Engaging style of presenting information	5	4	3	2	1
• Topics and activities have personal meaning and social relevance for students	5	4	3	2	1
• Allowance for curriculum differentiation for gifted learners	5	4	3	2	1

3. *Curriculum Responsiveness to Developmental Needs*

• Sequential exposure to language arts concepts from the concrete to the abstract	5	4	3	2	1
• Active engagement with language arts materials used to support the curriculum	5	4	3	2	1
• Sequential use of visual materials from the pictocentric to the text-centered	5	4	3	2	1
• Identified outcomes consonant with purpose	5	4	3	2	1

4. *Instructional Objectives*

• Clear and understandable	5	4	3	2	1
• Measurable	5	4	3	2	1
• Related to overall rationale and purpose	5	4	3	2	1

5. *Activities*

• Appropriate balance of teacher direction/student direction	5	4	3	2	1
• Developmentally appropriate activities	5	4	3	2	1
• Activities used to develop conceptual understanding	5	4	3	2	1
• Activities clarify, reinforce, and extend content	5	4	3	2	1
• Language arts integrated with other subjects	5	4	3	2	1

6. *Instructional Strategies*

• Varied strategies	5	4	3	2	1
• Opportunities for problem finding and solving	5	4	3	2	1
• Opportunities for open inquiry	5	4	3	2	1
• Varied grouping approaches including opportunities for small group and independent work	5	4	3	2	1
• Cooperative work focused on sharing multiple perspectives on issues	5	4	3	2	1
• Opportunities to practice decision-making strategies	5	4	3	2	1
• Use of various types of questions (e.g., convergent, divergent, evaluative)	5	4	3	2	1

7. *Assessment Procedures*

• Presence of pre- and postassessment measures	5	4	3	2	1
• Use of observational evaluation	5	4	3	2	1
• Use of authentic assessment	5	4	3	2	1
• Objective attainment assessment measures	5	4	3	2	1
• Assessment based on ability to get and use information	5	4	3	2	1
• Assessment based on outcomes of significance	5	4	3	2	1
• Opportunity for overall evaluation	5	4	3	2	1

8. *Materials/Resources*

• Instructional materials begin with students' current knowledge	5	4	3	2	1
• Supportive bibliography for teachers	5	4	3	2	1
• Frequent student misconceptions are identified for teachers	5	4	3	2	1
• Bibliography for student extension reading	5	4	3	2	1
• Supportive handout materials (informational worksheets, etc.)	5	4	3	2	1

9. *Extension Ideas*

• Worthwhile, related activities for students to pursue independently	5	4	3	2	1

10. *Technology Features (if applicable)*

• Actively engages students in higher order thinking skills and activities	5	4	3	2	1
• Enhances and complements instruction	5	4	3	2	1
• Provides effective interaction	5	4	3	2	1
• Allows exploration otherwise prohibited by time or money	5	4	3	2	1
• Provides access to resources that are unavailable in print, timely, or more comprehensive than media center printed materials	5	4	3	2	1
• Contains several levels of difficulty	5	4	3	2	1
• Provides useful, corrective feedback	5	4	3	2	1
• Easy to use	5	4	3	2	1
• Uncluttered screen design	5	4	3	2	1
• Lucid, economical text	5	4	3	2	1
• Dynamic visuals for abstract concepts	5	4	3	2	1
• Useful help screens	5	4	3	2	1
• Effective self-pacing devices	5	4	3	2	1
• Comprehensive teacher manual that includes instructions for use and modification, inventory, and specifications	5	4	3	2	1

Overall average score for Phase I review:______________________________

Comments on strengths/weaknesses:______________________________

Exemplary Language Arts Features: Phase II

Name of Reviewer: ______________________________

Title: ______________________________

Title of Curriculum to Be Reviewed: ______________________________

Appropriate Grade Level(s): ______________ Original Copyright Date: ______________

Date(s) of Revision: ______________________________

Directions:
Carefully read all curriculum materials and then rate the curriculum by each of the following criteria on a scale of: 5 = To an exemplary extent; 4 = To a good extent; 3 = Adequate; 2 = To a limited extent; and 1 = Not at all.

1. *Reading/Literature*

• Choice of literature	5	4	3	2	1
• Critical reading	5	4	3	2	1
• Textual analysis	5	4	3	2	1

2. *Multiculturalism/Globalism*

• Quality of material	5	4	3	2	1
• Balanced perspective	5	4	3	2	1
• Contributions of various cultural groups embedded	5	4	3	2	1

3. *Writing*

• Concept webbing	5	4	3	2	1
• Emphasis on different types of writing	5	4	3	2	1
• Use of writing strategies	5	4	3	2	1
• Use of revision	5	4	3	2	1
• Use of workshop techniques	5	4	3	2	1

4. *Language Study*

• Word relationships	5	4	3	2	1
• Vocabulary development	5	4	3	2	1
• Linguistic competence	5	4	3	2	1
• History of language	5	4	3	2	1
• Mechanics and usage	5	4	3	2	1

5. *Speaking/Listening Communication*

• Active engagement	5	4	3	2	1
• Opportunities for making oral presentations	5	4	3	2	1
• Causation	5	4	3	2	1
• Critical thinking	5	4	3	2	1

6. *Research Process*

• Provision of a model	5	4	3	2	1
• Issue/problem generation	5	4	3	2	1
• Development of research questions	5	4	3	2	1
• Broad-based communication	5	4	3	2	1

Overall average score for Phase II review:______________________________

Comments on strengths/weaknesses:______________________________

Tailoring for Special Populations: Phase III

Name of Reviewer: ______________________________

Title: ______________________________

Title of Curriculum to Be Reviewed: ______________________________

Appropriate Grade Level(s): ______________________________

Although curriculum may be found exemplary from a technical and even subject area perspective, it is important to consider the extent to which curriculum can be tailored to the needs of more targeted groups of learners with special needs. Thus the Phase III review process looks more closely at the features of exemplary curriculum for special populations.

Directions:
Carefully read all curriculum materials and then rate the curriculum by each of the following criteria on a scale of: 5 = To an exemplary extent; 4 = To a good extent; 3 = Adequate; 2 = To a limited extent; and 1 = Not at all.

Differentiation for High-Ability Learners

1. Provisions for acceleration and compression of content	5	4	3	2	1
2. Use of higher order thinking skills	5	4	3	2	1
3. Integration of content by key ideas, issues, and themes	5	4	3	2	1
4. Connection of ideas to other disciplines	5	4	3	2	1
5. Opportunities for advanced and broad-based reading	5	4	3	2	1
6. Use of multiple teaching resources	5	4	3	2	1
7. Use of diagnostic-prescriptive teaching	5	4	3	2	1
8. Attention to instructional pacing	5	4	3	2	1
9. Advanced reading level	5	4	3	2	1
10. Opportunities for students to develop advanced products	5	4	3	2	1
11. Opportunities for independent learning based on student ability and interest	5	4	3	2	1
12. Use of inquiry-based instructional techniques	5	4	3	2	1

Overall average score for Phase III review: ______________________________

Comments on strengths/weaknesses: ______________________________

References

Hirsch, E. D., Jr. (1987). *Cultural literacy: What every American needs to know.* Boston: Houghton Mifflin.

National Assessment Governing Board. (1992). *Reading framework for 1992 National Assessment of Education Progress.* Washington, DC: United States Department of Education.

National Council of Teachers of English and International Reading Association. (1996). *Standards for the English language arts.* Urbana, IL & Newark, DE: Authors.

Novak, J. D., & Gowin, D. B. (1984). *Learning how to learn.* NY: Cambridge University Press.

Spivey, N. (1990). Transforming texts. *Written Communication, 7,* 256–287.

Suhor, C. (1984). *1984 Report on trends and issues in English: A summary of reports from the NCTE commissions.* (ERIC Document Reproduction Service No. ED239290.)

Thompson, M. (1991). *The magic lens.* Unionville, NY: Trillium.

Tulley, M., & Farr, R. (1990). Textbook evaluation and selection. In D. L. Elliott and A. Woodward (Eds.), *Textbooks and schooling in the United States: Eighty-ninth yearbook of the National Society for the Study of Education, Part I* (pp. 162–177). Chicago: The National Society for the Study of Education, distributed by the University of Chicago Press.

VanTassel-Baska, J. (1992). *Planning effective curriculum for gifted learners.* Denver: Love.

VanTassel-Baska, J. (Ed.). (1994). *Comprehensive curriculum for gifted learners* (2nd ed.). Boston: Allyn & Bacon.

VanTassel-Baska, J., Johnson, D. T., & Boyce, L. N. (Eds.). (1996). *Developing verbal talent.* Boston: Allyn & Bacon.

References

SECTION 6

Frequently Asked Questions About the William & Mary Language Arts Curriculum

General Questions About Implementation of the William & Mary Language Arts Curriculum

We have been teaching the William & Mary units for several years. How do we keep the concept of change from getting stale and kids from being bored by the same activities?

Students bring something new to the process every year and change in their own understanding of the concept and the related lessons, so it's useful to go through again and allow them to see how they have grown in their thinking. Also, different nuances of change and how the generalizations are developed and applied can be emphasized from year to year. For example, the concept development activity can focus on changes in the individual in *Autobiographies and Memoirs,* or on changes in society in *Persuasion,* etc. The activity could also focus on specific forms of change, such as changes that happen in cycles in *Patterns of Change.* Students who have experienced multiple units and remember the generalizations from the beginning of the unit can review the generalizations and try to find new examples to support them, rather than reconstructing the generalizations. A lesson reintroducing the concept and the generalizations should be done at the beginning of every unit, but modifications of the types listed here can be done to keep the activity fresh for students who have experienced multiple units. Also, some teachers have suggested moving additional concept development work to the end of the unit for more experienced students, to enhance metacognition about unit learning.

How important are the unit selections?

None of the units is driven by an individual text. In all units, texts were selected for their rich language, complex ideas, multicultural perspectives, and thematic connections. Within each unit's sequence of lessons, the reading selections serve as the vehicle for thinking, discussion, and writing, providing opportunities to engage students in higher level thinking about significant, and sometimes controversial, issues. Alternative selections are recommended for students whose reading levels may be too low to handle advanced reading selections.

How are the readings in the program used?

The lessons at each grade level are purposefully designed to teach students to think critically about the issues raised by the texts. Through applying the Paul Reasoning Model in their questioning and in-class discussions, teachers encourage students to consider a variety of viewpoints, to distinguish between fact and opinion, and to make reasoned judgments supported by evidence. Over time, students refine their skills as they consistently apply this Reasoning Model to their reading, to their writing, and to their research. *More important than any individual text selection is the program's goal of teaching students to think critically by analyzing and interpreting what they read.*

Is the grammar packet the same or different in every unit?

There are two different grammar packets, one for upper elementary and one for middle school. The elementary one appears in *Literary Reflections, Autobiographies and Memoirs, Persuasion,* and *Patterns of Change.* The middle school one appears in *Utopia* and *The 1940s.* If students have done one of the packets in a previous year, we recommend giving them the pretest again to see if they have attained mastery, and then teaching or having them work independently with any sections needing additional attention. Also, the grammar section can be used as a resource by students; the grammar skills should be continually reinforced with the brief grammar activities within lessons and through a Language Study Learning Center. Teachers may also decide to give the middle school packet early to students who have already mastered the elementary packet.

What dictionaries should be used to support the vocabulary study?

All dictionaries are *not* created equal! It is important to keep in mind that the purpose of the Vocabulary Web is not to develop dictionary skills, but to develop vocabulary skills. It is more important to have a few good dictionaries in a classroom to be shared by students as they work with the Vocabulary Web than to have a class set of weaker dictionaries. The Vocabulary Web requires that a dictionary provide etymological information on words, such as stems, word origins, etc. A dictionary that provides as much of this information as possible is preferable. In the resource section of each unit, the dictionaries we recommend are listed. Since the publication of the units, additional resources have become available online; for example, students can access Merriam-Webster entries on line at www.m-w.com, and the *American Heritage* is one of the dictionaries used as a resource at www.dictionary.com. For teachers of primary students, also consider the option of excerpting relevant definitions from the recommended dictionaries for students to use rather than confronting them with dictionaries they can't lift. Once again, the purpose is not to find out if they can use guide words, etc.; access to the entries is the important thing.

Why are mechanics not addressed in the writing rubric?

The units are not focused on usage, punctuation, spelling, capitalization, or other details of mechanics. Our intent in using the rubrics for the writing pre- and posttest is to measure student growth in persuasive writing skills. Certainly, it is important for students to develop good writing mechanics; other writing activities throughout the units emphasize the writing process, including careful editing. However, we did not make it a focus of the rubric because it is not the purpose of the test. Teachers may decide to grade the tests for mechanics, but we would encourage this part of the grade to be considered separately from the rubric score so that you may appropriately measure their growth in persuasive writing.

How do I get students to read their peers' work critically instead of them just saying, "My friend's paper is excellent, of course!"?

In the middle school units, we added "accountability" pieces to the self- and peer writing assessments within the units. For example, if students are saying the peer's main idea is clear, they are asked to state the main idea on the form. If they are saying strong vocabulary is used, they are asked to list a few effective words and phrases. These more specific requirements for peer editing can also be required of elementary students that are capable of handling them.

Our school district does not want to use a particular book. What do we do to replace it?

The books in these units were very carefully chosen according to specific criteria, and we feel that they are thought-provoking and important books for high-ability students to read. We strongly recommend that teachers read all the literature pieces carefully before teaching them and that school districts examine the texts according to their literature approval policies. In cases in which a book cannot be used at a certain grade level or is not allowed to be used in the district, we recommend that teachers examine the list of criteria for literature selection given in this book to find a replacement title.

Can I use these units with my students who are not identified as gifted? It seems that many of the activities in these units would be good for all students.

We feel that the organization of the units and several of the teaching models included may be effective with students other than high-ability groups. We have several sites in which teachers use all of the models with all of their students to some degree. If teachers are going to try to use the models with all students, we recommend that they (a) use the Literature Web but with different literature selections for average-ability students, (b) use extra reinforcement for the Reasoning Model, (c) vary the prompts for writing and the requirements for writing format (paragraph, essay, etc.), and (d) allow gifted students to work together in groups for group activities rather than making small groups heterogeneous.

Can the program be adjusted or tiered to meet the needs of all learners?

Yes. Teachers can adjust the content by selecting alternate texts. They can differentiate the process by varying the intensity and complexity of tasks to encourage participation of all students in some components of the program. Suggested adjustments can be found in the following sections of this guide:

- Differentiation for high-ability learners (pages 15–16)
- Instructional support for special needs learners (pages 39–43)

What's the time frame for implementation of the units?

We estimate that full implementation would be 40 to 50 hours of instructional time, ideally spread across a semester of the school year. The units can constitute a significant portion of a language arts program for high-ability students in a district, supplemented by other strong materials for the other portions of the year. In addition, we recommend using the teaching models beyond the context of the units. It may even be useful to introduce some of the models before you start the units so that students are familiar with their use before they are faced with them all at once.

Is professional development on implementing the units available?

Professional development opportunities related to the Center's curriculum are available periodically at the College and may also be arranged for local school districts through our Center. Please call 757-221-2588 for information.

What would an observer expect to see?

An observer should see the integration of content, process, and concept development in any lesson. Students should be involved in inquiry-based learning, reflected in high-level discussion, writing, or research activities. Instruction and assignments should emphasize key concepts, themes, and ideas.

Pages 47–50 provide the observation instrument to be used for assessing implementation. This involves observing teacher behaviors in the classroom. A teacher log also allows for notations on each lesson taught.

Using the William & Mary Curriculum in Special Programs and Alternative Settings

Can I use the William & Mary curriculum units in a home school environment?

The William & Mary language arts units have been used by a number of families in the home school environment. It requires some revision on the part of the parent, because the units do emphasize small and large group interaction among students, but the units are definitely usable in home school settings, especially the language arts and social studies units.

We recommend attending one of our implementation workshops for training in implementing the units because we model the teaching practices that are incorporated in the units, and we try to address the questions that we know will arise when you start working through the units. The training is not required but most instructors find it helpful, as do parents who home school their children. We have workshops available in each curriculum strand. We hold training sessions at William & Mary several times a year; specifically, there is a one-day workshop in March during the preconference session of our National Curriculum Network Conference (NCNC), and a three-day workshop in June at our Summer Institute. We also conduct workshops for school districts around the country. For more information, contact us at cfge@wm.edu.

What modifications will I need to make to use the William & Mary curriculum units in a home school environment?

Most modifications required to use the William & Mary curriculum units in a home school environment relate to the time required for implementation, grade level specifications, and grouping for instructional activities.

The units vary in the recommended allotment of time for implementation. In a classroom setting, the language arts units are usually used for a semester. All of the units are designed to be somewhat flexible for the teacher; they can really be as long or short as you'd like them to be. They all include lesson extensions, suggestions for Learning Centers, and other explorations in addition to the regular lessons.

Our grade level indicators are intended to refer to highly able students at the grade level specified. For example, a unit for Grades 4 to 5 means the unit is appropriate for gifted fourth and fifth graders. You can start at whatever level seems appropriate for your child. The reading selections and activities are all pitched two or three years above-average grade level, and the teaching models are the same across all units. Contact our publisher, Kendall Hunt (http://www.kendallhunt.com), to request a review copy to examine before purchasing if you want to determine which unit would be best for your child. Or, if you attend any of our professional development events at William & Mary, we also have copies of materials available for examination.

Implementing the curriculum units would also require some tailoring of the instructional activities because the lessons reference "putting students into groups." The language arts and social studies units specify pairings and small group discussion to compare/contrast ideas and understanding.

Language Arts Resources for Teachers

SECTION 7

This list includes both resources related to language arts instruction and materials that may be used to supplement the William & Mary language arts units.

Art Resources

Appel, A., Jr. (1992). *The art of celebration: Twentieth-century painting, literature, sculpture, photography, and jazz.* NY: Alfred A. Knopf.

Bonafoux, P. (1985). *Portraits of the artist: The self-portrait in painting.* NY: Rizzoli.

Dallas Museum of Art. (1989). *Ancestral legacy: The African impulse in African-American art.* Dallas, TX: Author.

Feder, N. (1965). *American Indian art.* NY: Harry N. Abrams.

Furst, P. T., & Furst, J. L. (1982). *North American Indian art.* NY: Rizzoli.

Highwater, J. (1978). *Many smokes, many moons: A chronology of American Indian history through Indian art.* Philadelphia: J. B. Lippincott Company.

Highwater, J. (1983). *Arts of the Indian Americans: Leaves from the sacred tree.* NY: Harper & Row.

Janson, A. F. (2003). *History of art for young people* (6th ed.). NY: Prentice Hall.

Janson, A. F. (2006). *Janson's history of art* (7th ed.). NY: Prentice Hall.

National Museum of Women in the Arts. (1987). *Women in the arts.* NY: Harry N. Abrams.

Roalf, P. (1993). *Looking at paintings: Self-portraits.* NY: Hyperion.

Van Devanter, A. C., & Frankenstein, A. V. (1974). *American self-portraits, 1670–1973.* Washington, DC: International Exhibitions Foundation.

Concept Development

Müller, J. (1973). *The changing countryside.* NY: Atheneum.

Müller, J. (1976). *The changing city.* NY: Atheneum.

Taba, H. (1962). *Curriculum development: Theory and practice.* NY: Harcourt, Brace & World.

Curriculum Resources

Marzano, R. J., Pickering, D. J., Arrendondo, D. E., Blackburn, G. J., Brandt, R. S., & Moffett, C. A. (1997). *Dimensions of learning: Teacher's manual.* (2nd ed.). Alexandria, VA: Association for Supervision and Curriculum Development.

Taba, H. (1962). *Curriculum development: Theory and practice.* NY: Harcourt, Brace & World.

VanTassel-Baska, J. (1992). *Planning effective curriculum for gifted learners.* Denver, CO: Love Publishing.

VanTassel-Baska, J. (1998). *Excellence in educating gifted learners* (3rd ed.). Denver, CO: Love Publishing.

VanTassel-Baska, J. (2003). *Curriculum planning and instructional design for gifted learners.* Denver, CO: Love Publishing.

VanTassel-Baska, J., Johnson, D. T., & Boyce, L. N. (Eds.). (1996). *Developing verbal talent.* Boston: Allyn & Bacon.

VanTassel-Baska, J., & Little, C. (Eds.). (2010). *Content-based curriculum for gifted learners* (2nd ed.). Waco, TX: Prufrock.

VanTassel-Baska, J., & Stambaugh, T. (2006). *Comprehensive curriculum for gifted learners* (3rd ed.). Needham Heights, MA: Allyn & Bacon.

Dictionaries

Houghton Mifflin. (2006). *American heritage dictionary of the English language* (4th ed.). Boston: Author.

Merriam-Webster. (2003). *Merriam-Webster's collegiate dictionary* (11th ed.). Springfield, MA: Author.

Language Arts Skills Development Resources (Including: Comprehension, Critical Thinking, Reasoning, Research, and Speaking Skills)

Boyce, L. N. (1997). *A guide to teaching research skills and strategies in grades 4–12.* Williamsburg, VA: Center for Gifted Education.

Costa, A. L. (Ed.). (1991). *Developing minds* (Rev. ed., Vol. 1–2). Alexandria, VA: Association for Supervision and Curriculum Development.

Kaufer, D. S., Geisler, C. D., & Neuwirth, C. M. (1989). *Arguing from sources.* NY: Harcourt Brace Jovanovich.

Kaye, S. M., & Thomson, P. (2007). *Philosophy for teens: Questioning life's big ideas.* Waco, TX: Prufrock Press, Inc.

Langrehr, J. (1988). *Teaching students to think.* Bloomington, IN: National Education Service.

Lipson, G. B., & Greenberg, B. N. (1981). *Extra! Extra! Read all about it: How to use the newspaper in the classroom.* Carthage, IL: Good Apple.

Lucas, S. E. (1986). *The art of public speaking.* NY: Random House.

Marzano, R. J. (1992). *Cultivating thinking in English.* Urbana, IL: National Council of Teachers of English.

Miller, R. K. (1992). *The informed argument: A multidisciplinary reader and guide* (3rd ed.). Fort Worth, TX: Harcourt Brace Jovanovich.

Minn, L. B. (1982). *Teach speech: Oral presentation strategies.* Carthage, IL: Good Apple.

Norton, D. E. (1982). Using a webbing process to develop children's literature units. *Language Arts, 59,* 348–356.

Parnes, S. J. (1975). *Aha! Insights into creative behavior.* Buffalo, NY: DOK Publishers.

Paul, R. (1992). *Critical thinking: What every person needs to survive in a rapidly changing world.* Sonoma, CA: The Foundation for Critical Thinking.

Paul, R., Binker, A. J. A., Jensen, K., & Kreklau, H. (1990). *Critical thinking handbook: 4th–6th grades, a guide for remodeling lesson plans in language arts, social studies, and science.* Rohnert Park, CA: Sonoma State University, Foundation for Critical Thinking.

Polette, N. (2001). *The research book for gifted programs.* (Rev. ed.). Marion, IL: Pieces of Learning.

Rottenberg, A. T. (1991). *Elements of argument: A text and reader* (3rd ed.). Boston: Bedford Books of St. Martin's Press.

Ryan, M. (1987). *So you have to give a speech!* NY: Franklin Watts.

Swicord, B. (1984). Debating with gifted fifth and sixth graders—Telling it like it was, is, and could be. *Gifted Child Quarterly, 28,* 127–129.

Thomson, P. (2009). *The old testament for teens: A guide to critical issues and perspectives.* Waco, TX: Prufrock Press, Inc.

Toulmin, S., Rieke, R., & Janik, A. (1979). *An introduction to reasoning.* NY: Macmillan.

VanTassel-Baska, J., & Stambaugh, T. (2008). *Jacob's Ladder, Volumes I–III.* Waco, TX: Prufrock Press.

White, D. A. (2005). *Examined life: Advanced philosophy for kids.* Waco, TX: Prufrock Press, Inc.

Learning Theories Resources

Donovan, M. S., & Bransford, J.D. (Eds.). (2005). *How students learn.* Washington, DC: The National Academies Press.

Novak, J. D., & Gowin, D. B. (1984). *Learning how to learn.* NY: Cambridge University Press.

Literature and Reading Resources

Baskin, B. H., & Harris, K. H. (1980). *Books for the gifted child.* NY: Bowker.

Center for Gifted Education. (2002). *Navigator Series.* Williamsburg, VA: Author.

Duggan, T. J. (2008). *Advanced placement classroom: Hamlet.* Waco, TX: Prufrock Press, Inc.

Elliot, E. (Ed.). (1991). *American literature: A Prentice Hall anthology.* Englewood, NJ: Prentice Hall.

Halsted, J. W. (2002). *Some of my best friends are books: Guiding gifted readers from pre-school to high school* (2nd ed.). Scottsdale, AZ: Gifted Potential Press, Inc.

Johnson, K. L., & Heinemann, L. (2008). *Advanced placement classroom: A midsummer night's dream.* Waco, TX: Prufrock Press, Inc.

Lampert, R. B. (2008). *Advanced placement classroom: Romeo and Juliet.* Waco, TX: Prufrock Press, Inc.

Thompson, M. C. (1995). *Classics in the classroom.* Unionville, NY: Royal Fireworks Press.

Vocabulary Resources

Reading Manipulatives. (n.d.). *Latin roots match-ups.* Phoenix, AZ: Author.

Thompson, M. C. (1995). *Word within the word III* (2nd ed.). Unionville, NY: Royal Fireworks Press.

Thompson, M. C. (2001). *Caesar's English I* (2nd ed.). Unionville, NY: Royal Fireworks Press.

Thompson, M. C. (2003). *Caesar's English II* (2nd ed.). Unionville, NY: Royal Fireworks Press.

Thompson, M. C. (2003). *Word within the word I* (2nd ed.). Unionville, NY: Royal Fireworks Press.

Thompson, M. C. (2003). *Word within the word II* (2nd ed.). Unionville, NY: Royal Fireworks Press.

Writing Resources

Bradbury, R. (1990). *Zen and the art of writing.* Santa Barbara, CA: Capra Press.

Burkhalter, N. (1995). A Vygotsky-based curriculum for teaching persuasive writing in the elementary grades. *Language Arts, 72,* 192–196.

McKeague, P. (2010). *Writing about literature: Step by step* (9th ed.). Dubuque, IA: Kendall Hunt Publishing Company.

Thompson, M. C. (2001). *Magic lens I* (2nd ed.). Unionville, NY: Royal Fireworks Press.

Thompson, M. C. (2002). *Grammar island.* Unionville, NY: Royal Fireworks Press.

Thompson, M. C. (2002). *Magic lens II* (2nd ed.). Unionville, NY: Royal Fireworks Press.

Thompson, M. C. (2003). *Grammar town.* Unionville, NY: Royal Fireworks Press.

Thompson, M. C. (2003). *Grammar voyage.* Unionville, NY: Royal Fireworks Press.

Thompson, M. C. (2003). *Magic lens III.* Unionville, NY: Royal Fireworks Press.

Tiedt, I. M. (1989). *Writing: From topic to evaluation.* Boston: Allyn & Bacon.

INDEX

N

O

P

Q

R

S

T

U

V

W

Printed in the USA
CPSIA information can be obtained
at www.ICGtesting.com
LVHW061311280824
789490LV00001B/5

9 780757 5648